I0043909

THE
PEOPLE
FACTOR

THE
PEOPLE
FACTOR

The Next Leap in
Project Management

Sonja van Uden

Madison **+** Park

A Global Branding Agency

Copyright © 2019 Sonja van Uden
Written by Sonja van Uden
Edited by Dylan Garity

Illustrations by:
Judith Oosterom
Patrick Harding
Scott Webb
JJ Jordan
Sonja van Uden
Tineke Vonk

Published by Madison + Park
Executive Assistant: Fahtema Lewis
Project Manager: Casene Goulbourne
Brand Strategist: Rahfeal Gordon

All rights reserved. No part of this book may be reproduced, stored, or transmitted by any means—whether auditory, graphic, mechanical, or electronic—without written permission of both publisher and author, except in the case of brief excerpts used in critical articles and reviews. Unauthorized reproduction of any part of this work is illegal and is punishable by law.

978-0-9978311-4-6 (Hardcover)
978-0-9978311-5-3 (Softcover)

Because of the dynamic nature of the Internet, any web addresses or links contained in this book may have changed since publication and may no longer be valid. The views expressed in this work are solely those of the author and do not necessarily reflect the views of the publisher, and the publisher hereby disclaims any responsibility for them.

Published 2019
United States of America

*To my parents, Mariska & Paul, who
instilled in me a curiosity for life and its wonder. Who,
without judgment, walked alongside me during every
adventure I have been on. I could not have done it
without you.*

#familyiseverything #curiosityforlife

CONTENTS

FOREWORD

How can you translate the business strategy to your team if management is unclear about the objective? How can you ensure a client of an on-time delivery six months from now if you don't even know what tomorrow will bring? How can you deal with a new conflict in your team if you haven't dealt with one like it before?

These examples are more fact than fiction for the ever-growing collective of project managers in the world today. Each day, these managers make a conscious decision to step into the ambiguity of the project arena, which is turning progressively more complex. In projects, everything is connected with everything else, and predictions made today can be worthless by tonight. It takes the right intentions and attitude to keep working toward the achievement of the goal, over and over again.

Project management methods today deal mostly with the whats and hows of projects. Rational and tangible aspects, such as the budget, schedule and risk management, are well-researched and form the curricula of dozens of project-management courses and programs worldwide. Yet, failure in projects is often not related to these factors but rather to the timeless principles of working with people.

The People Factor teaches project professionals the skills to deal with the whoms and whens of projects instead. These skills are necessary to building connectivity and trust between people. This leads to a shared mindset in which successes are celebrated and frustrations and burdens are carried together. These skills establish a never-wavering commitment toward project success.

For the analytical project professional, this might take some effort to get used to. There's no dashboard or spreadsheet, but rather seven action-focused skills, like understand, adapt and know, that will help you influence your own attitude and behavior as well as those of others. Each skill has been thoroughly researched and enriched with suggestions and examples from a group of fifty practicing project professionals, who were brutally honest and vulnerable in relating their experiences.

I know it still might sound daunting. I hear you thinking, "Nothing is as fickle as human behavior." And that's true. However, it is increasingly clear that these clearly discernible disciplines are non-negotiable and mission-critical.

Without the incorporation of the seven skills of the People Factor even the best-designed project, with all the most-critical, traditional best practices applied, will stand less than a 30-percent[1] chance of achieving their goals. Figures by the Project Management Institute show $122 million of every $1 billion that companies spend on projects is wasted due to poor performance. This means the total waste on projects in the US alone is somewhere in the neighborhood of $150 billion each year.

This book seeks to significantly decrease the over-70-percent probability of failed expectations, and increase the possibility of success, by incorporating the People Factor.

Seventy-three percent of schedules on Oil & Gas projects are delayed (EY, 2014).

Seventy percent of ICT projects are not a success (Standish Group, 1994, 1999, 2004, 2009).

Eight out of ten innovation projects are called 'a failure' (Harkema, 2003).

There is a 50- to 100-percent time and cost overrun in infrastructural projects (Hertogh & Westerveld, 2010).

Sixty-five percent of mega-projects don't achieve the purpose of the organization (Merrow, 2011).

Transportation projects have a 55-percent cost overrun. (INDOT, 2004)

1. *Failure figures on projects in technical industries.*

ABOUT THE AUTHOR

Driving home one Friday evening, I decided I'd had enough. With another weekend spent alone ahead of me, I knew that something needed to change. I was sick of feeling lonely. If I did not change something fast, my adventure abroad wouldn't last much longer. I'd been living in Norway for a little over nine months by then.

One year later, my life looked completely different. I was spending weekends in the mountains with colleagues and building a small but steady group of friends around me to hang out with. My adventure turned from misery into the best thing that's ever happened to me. And as a by-product, I've become an increasingly more success-ful project manager as well.

My passion for projects started before I moved to Norway. I love the fast-paced, high-pressure arena of projects, the technical landscape of some of the sectors I've been working in, and project management as a discipline-originated from. I've accumulated over fifteen years of practical experience as a project professional. I've managed projects from client, contractor and supplier perspectives. I've led project departments. As an entrepreneur, I build up project organizations and standardized project processes. And most recently, I completed academic research into effectiveness amongst project managers. All of this led me to the profound and vital belief that projects are as much about people as they are about anything else.

Before anything else, we all strive to have an enjoyable life. For most of us in the Western world, this includes taking up a profession and spending the majority of our adult life at work. We hope that we can do something enjoyable that won't feel like a 'have-to' most of the time. I know that projects are demanding and ambiguous. But I promise you, there is still space for enjoying the rollercoaster ride together. Through this book, I will give you insights and tools to put some of the joy back in the projects you engage in. I will help you give purpose and meaning to the shared, epic quest that is a project. Enjoy!

Sonja van Uden

INTRODUCTION

I t is almost impossible today to pick up a newspaper or business journal and not read something about projects. Organizations worldwide use projects for tactical or strategic reasons, to satisfy customer needs and drive business value. Millions of people around the world consider project management to be their main profession. We have become a project-oriented society.

Projects, in one form or another, have been around for as long as humans have been. Project-based endeavors were seen in the form of worship, engineering, and even nation-building, with the people controlling them being generals, priests or architects, each focusing on a specific calling. Most of these projects were successfully completed despite uncertainties that could have ensured their failure. Examples of great historic projects are the Great Wall of China, the silk route connecting Asia and Europe, and the Battle of Gettysburg, to name a few.

> "All of mankind's greatest accomplishments—from building the great pyramids to discovering a cure for polio to putting a man on the moon—began as a project."
> —*Project Management: The Managerial Process*

Around the 1950s, various technical industries came together to establish the first project-management methods. They build a toolbox of best practices, which was solely based on the idea that the goal of a project was straightforward and clear at the very begin-ning. For example, "build a bridge over a river" or "build a factory according to certain requirements."

Since then, all kinds of industries and disciplines have started calling all kinds of things projects: merger and acquisition, gov-ernment tasks, start-up building, research, even change within organizations. All of these projects are executed using the same his-torical project management toolbox, which is dominated by tools for controlling the project based on the presumption the outcome is clear from the start. Various studies, however, show significant failure of projects across the board, independent of discipline or industry. The Oil and Gas industry, for example, shows 64-percent cost overruns and 73-percent schedule delays (EY, 2014). In the IT field, 70 percent of projects are unsuccessful (Standish Group, 2009). And these are only a few of the staggering failure figures out there (see table on page xi). Why? I wondered over and over again. Time to investigate.

Organizations

The engine of almost any organization in the world today runs on a combination of business-as-usual and projects. Business-as-usual signifies the execution of standard functional operations within the organization. These are the things that keep the lights on—they operate through cyclic work processes and have predefined budgets and targets. Examples of business-as-usual in organizations include administration, human resources and asset management. Projects, on the other hand, are specific endeavors to accomplish specific things. Although projects have long been a style of doing business in technical industries, nowadays projects have spread to all avenues of work. They are a means to get things done—anything from a factory expansion to upgrading an information system or solving social problems. There are a number of additional significant differences between project work and business-as-usual:

A project is temporary. Each project has a distinct beginning and end, which is measured in time. The duration of a project might be three days, or it might span multiple years. Business-as-usual does not stop—it remains ongoing. It produces ongoing work with no foreseeable end date.

A project is unique or has one or more unique elements, which brings with it inevitable risk. In projects, this risk is managed to get to the best possible outcome. Business-as-usual seeks to mitigate all risk to reach operational excellence, with a goal of taking all uncertainty out of repeatable processes to reach organizational stability.

The design of project teams is hugely different from business-as-usual teams. Project teams consist of cross-functional experts who are put in positions with distinct responsibilities to deliver a particular output. Main roles in project teams include the project manager, customer, and supplier, as well as subject matter experts. Business-as-usual, on the other hand, consists of functional teams, experts in their own right who are grouped together in a division.

The distribution between business-as-usual and projects amongst organizations differs significantly. Some organizations depend largely on business-as-usual for revenue streams while only using projects for strategical purposes. Other organizations largely create revenue through projects and only use business-as-usual for overhead purposes. Still others are positioned somewhere in-between. For all, however, it is undeniable that stability and sustainability depend on the successful execution of both business-as-usual and projects.

Projects

Projects are ways to get things done and can be classified as either being strategic, operational or sales. Strategic projects are endeavors to maintain the competitive position of the organization. They can include purchasing a new company or developing a new product. Operational projects are endeavors to help the organization improve existing processes. Implementation of a new customer relations system or lean implementation are examples of operational projects. Sales projects are specific contracts with customers to produce a unique product or service. All three classes of projects are vitally important to an organization's sustainability.

Projects are run by project teams, which can take up various positions within a company structure. Project teams come in all shapes and sizes and consist of a number of vital roles, such as the project manager, the project coordinator, and subject matter experts. Project professionals aren't afraid to take on a challenge and bring to the table a mindset of getting things done.

The project manager is responsible for the joint effort of reaching the project objective. It isn't uncommon for a project manager to be responsible for a group of professionals they have never worked with before and have no hierarchical authority over. Together with the ambiguity and demand of a project, this is not a role for the timid, as you can imagine. Although everyone can develop skills to manage projects, there is something specific about having the right mixture of traits and temperament, aka nature, to effectively fulfill the requirements of the job. The most important aspects are:

- If you don't like working with others, managing projects is not for you. The success of a project depends on the commitment and joint effort of the entire team and is set up for failure without it.

- If you have difficulties handling change, managing projects is not for you either. Projects are ambiguous, and things rarely go according to plan. You need to be comfortable with improvising and adapting whenever the project demands it.

- The sheer volume of things going on simultaneously in projects can be overwhelming. If you have difficulties finding the important signals that exist in the midst of all the noise, projects are not for you either.

Each project is a joint endeavor of professionals in different roles with different responsibilities, with the main purpose of accomplishing a pre-set goal over time, contributing to the stability and sustainability of an organization. These professionals can be educated in the field of project management, or they can just be people with the right mindset to get things done.

Project management

Project management today is the result of a natural evolution in which, incremental with every project, best practices advanced, paving the way for the next historical project. Around the 1950s, the demand from technical industries for more advanced methods to cope with the growing complexity and size of projects resulted in the inception of the very first project management institutes and written-down project management methods. Some of these institutes are still around today, like the International Project Management Association (IPMA), which was formed in Austria, and the Project Management Institute (PMI), which was founded in the United States. In 1987, the Project Management Institute released the Project Management Book of Knowledge, which since has become the global standard, with over 5.5 million copies circulated worldwide. Both institutes educate an extensive number of project professionals each year.

In the 1970s, the progression of computers facilitated the emergence of various project management software companies and tools. Out of demand from this industry emerged the Scrum method and the Agile Manifesto, both written and introduced in the information technology field. Other project methods in use today are Kanban, Lean, Waterfall, Design Thinking, and Prince2.

Analyzing the natural evolution of best practices results in an accumulation of formal, purely logical whats and hows. The following are the most commonly used:

- The **budget** is the financial framework of the project and is established to estimate the total cost of the project. Large projects can have budgets that are several pages long and include labor costs, material costs and operating costs. The project budget is a great tool for the project team to not only determine cost but also manage it over time. Throughout the project lifespan, the budget is continuously checked and updated.

- The **schedule** is a timetable of the project and is established to determine the project's total duration. It contains the work that needs to be performed, which resources of the project team will perform which parts of the work, and the timeframes in which those parts need to be completed. The schedule reflects all of the work associated with delivering the project on time. The ability to set up a practical schedule requires extensive experience on scope breakdowns.

- The **work breakdown structure** (WBS for short) is a framework to break down the scope of a project. The work breakdown structure is commonly visualized in a hierarchical tree structure that outlines the project and breaks it down into smaller, manageable components. It is a great way to divide and conquer large project scopes, making them more manageable.

- The **critical path analysis** (CPA) is a tool that determines the longest path of a project. It calculates when the earliest and latest activities can start and finish without expanding the project's overall timeline. Critical path analysis is a widely used project management tool to help project professionals handle complex and time-sensitive projects.

- **Variation** control is a common concept in projects and a way of managing slippage of the project scope. A variation is defined as an actual condition that is entirely different from the expected condition, which is commonly contained within the budget and the schedule. Variations can consist of costs, durations, and amounts of resources available. The management of variations is mostly the responsibility of the project manager and requires a well-established and maintained budget, schedule and work breakdown structure.

- The **metrics** dashboard or key performance indicator dashboard (KPI), is a tool to quantify the effectiveness to which a project reaches its objective(s). Metrics are defined at the start of a project and are typically linked to various milestones in the schedule. Metrics are commonly used as a reporting tool to both internal management and external clients.

- **Outsourcing** allows the project to subcontract parts of the scope to third parties. Procurement is a well-known outsourcing tool for buying goods or services. The project manager usually determines what and when to outsource within the limits of the project.

- **Risk management** is a framework for monitoring and controlling risks and opportunities during the lifecycle of a project. A register is maintained in which the identification, evaluation and prioritization of risks and opportunities are coordinated. It is key that the probability and impact are quantified so that possible threats or opportunities can be managed appropriately. The project team requires expertise and experience to set up and maintain a realistic and practical risk register.

- **Quality** control is a bit of an odd duck and not always available in projects. However, especially in the technical industry, it is a huge part of project delivery. Quality control consists of observation techniques and activities used to evaluate whether a product or service has measured up to the upfront-specified requirements. Quality control requires specific knowledge and experience from project professionals.

All of the above best practices have been developed over the last seventy years and form the curricula for dozens of project management courses and programs worldwide. Young professionals who want to enter the project management field take part in these courses and programs, believing this will equip them to manage

projects. My own experi-
ence and conversations with
project professionals over
many years, however, have
taught me differently. Each
project is a joint endeavor
of people, and the shared
mindset and commitment
of these people is the key to
project success. None of the

work
breakdown
structure

metrics

variation

critical
path
analysis

budget   quality

risk   schedule   outsourcing

mentioned best practices influences this shared mindset or commitment. Not convinced yet? Let's look at some examples of what
I mean:

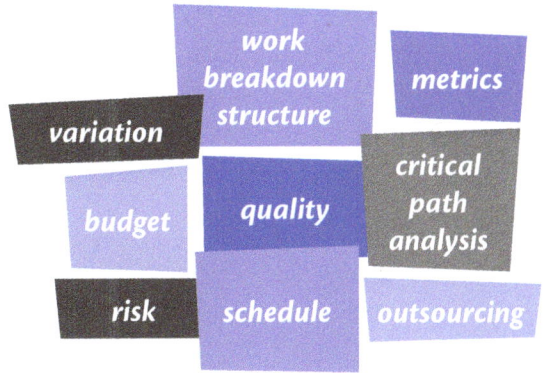

> You are working on a strategic project within your
> organization. The plan is to implement a new logistics soft-
> ware to group together some of the outdated systems used
> within the company today. The project is a brilliant idea,
> and the business case supporting headcount and cost has
> been approved by the board of directors. You are excited
> to work with Peter, who has been assigned as the project
> sponsor, and the two of you immediately start working
> on the project with the rest of the project team. Together,
> you establish the scope, plan and budget, and start roll-
> ing out the project. Along the way, you encounter massive
> resistance from the logistics department. They are not
> onboard when it comes to the change-out of the system,
> and on several occasions they refrain from providing the
> necessary information to complete the design of the new
> software. The project team gets frustrated, as the required
> work is falling behind. You knew this was one of the risks
> you might encounter. You qualified and quantified it in the

*first risk session you ran together with the team and have
on several occasions spoken with Peter to mitigate the risk.
Peter committed to 'selling' the change within the logistics
department, but by the looks of it he wasn't successful (yet).*

In the above example, the project is making use of traditional
best practices. The scope has been established. A schedule and
budget have been established and are being used, and risks have
been established and are being mitigated. Still, the job doesn't seem
to be getting done, and the project is slipping. Why?

Let's look at another example:

*You are working on a design, engineering and procure-
ment contract for a company in the oil industry. You have
run similar contracts like this before and are confident in
reaching an on-time and within-budget delivery. You are
halfway into the project when an engineer in a vital role
has a car accident. He is down with a complicated bone
fracture for at least the next five months. You get assigned
a new engineer who starts off proactively digging into the
agreed scope, the schedule, the engineering budget, the risk
register and the already-completed design work. You get
her up to speed as fast as you can to ensure no further
delays on the design work. After a week, you get a big surprise. The new engineer discovers that the current design
ever-so-slightly differs from the agreed-upon scope requirements. You calculate that if you have to stick to the change,
you will overrun the project budget by almost 7 percent.
You take part in the next engineering meeting between the
internal engineers and the client team and bring up the
subject. The meeting ends in a disagreement between you*

and the client lead engineer, which needs to be resolved. You request a meeting with the client straight away. You prepare and arm yourself for a tough conversation, targeting a reversal of the current design. After you state your case, the client hands you an email, in which the engineer who fell ill agreed to the design change, at no additional cost. What now? you think, trying to contain your anger.

Again, the project is making use of the traditional best practices like the scope breakdown, budget and schedule, but still, challenges remain. What should you use from the best practices toolbox to resolve these challenges? And, if the best practices toolbox does not suffice, then what is missing?

The People Factor

The People Factor is an invitation into skills for project professionals to successfully influence the people side of projects. These are elementary skills that establish a shared mindset to deal with the demand and ambiguity of the project together and to make the achievement of the project goal the joint priority of everyone involved.

I have established a framework to introduce seven skills that, based on my research, are fundamentally valuable. They are directed at either yourself, others, or both, and they will incite action within the project. These seven skills are are shown on the next page.

- Know

- Communicate

- Socialize

- Adapt

- Understand

- Motivate

- Lead

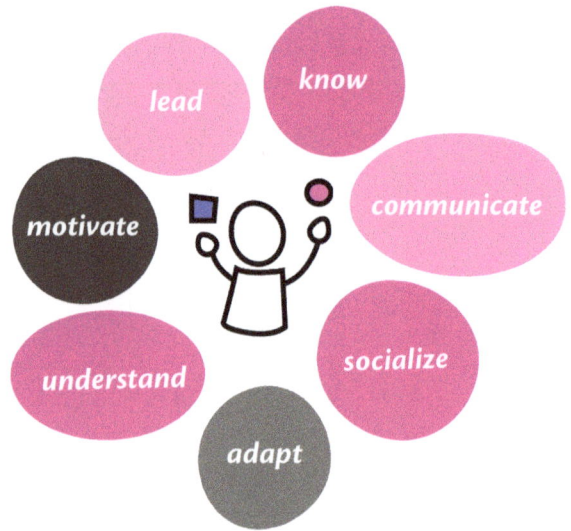

With these seven skills of the People Factor now defined, let's look back at the two examples from practice I mentioned before. In the first example, you are working together with the project team on the implementation of a new software system for the logistical department. Peter has not been able to get the department onboard, and there is resistance to cooperate. Let's analyze how some of the seven skills of the People Factor can be put to use without even going into further detail on them:

- The excitement about working with Peter could have clouded your judgement of his ability to get the necessary support from the logistics department. Knowing Peter's strengths and weaknesses could have resulted in a better cooperation between the two teams. You need the **know** skill of the People Factor. To resolve this situation, you need to adjust your approach to the logistics department, which means you need the skill to **adapt**.

- The project team is frustrated about the behavior of the logistics department. Their willingness to cooperate remains key for the project to succeed. You need to appeal to their individual or collective drives to keep them committed. You need the skill to **motivate**.

- The behavior of the logistics department is a risk to the successful implementation and use of the new software. You will have to talk to Peter and perhaps even the board to get them onboard—you will need to **communicate**.

The second example from practice can be analyzed in the same way. You need to understand the impact of the loss of the engineer on the project team and allow space to grieve, which is part of **understand**. You need to get the new engineer up to speed and get her committed to the end-goal, for which you need to **lead**. You need to welcome her and make sure she feels part of the team quickly. For this, you and you team need to **socialize**. You need to **adapt** to the new variation issue you are dealing with, which is fairly impossible if you can't control your own emotions. And finally, you need to negotiate with the client to get it resolved, for which you need to **communicate**. All of these are skills that incite action and are not part of the traditional best practices, but they are critical to achieving project success.

> *Pant and Baroudi write, in the* **International Journal of Project Management,** *"The project management discipline still appears to place greater emphasis on hard skills at the expense of the softer human skills. Evidence to support this conclusion can be seen in body of knowledge guides such as that of PMBOK as well as the program syllabi of many educational providers of project management studies. There are a growing number of those that are critical in respect*

> to the sustainability of such substantially hard approaches to project management. The criticism is not in respect to the teaching of technical skills within project management but rather the lack of emphasis on the human side. A more balanced approach between hard and soft concepts would see them complementing each other and enhancing project management education in the process."

A necessary marriage

Every day of a project is different, and each project challenge needs its own approach. By breaking down the two examples into the use of both best practices and the People Factor's skills, I hope to have given you a better understanding of how everything in a project is intertwined and connected. Perhaps you do not like the phrase 'necessary marriage,' but it is a great way to describe the connection. To maximize your influence on the successful outcome of a project, you need both the logical and rational whats and whos of projects as well as the timeless principles of working with people.

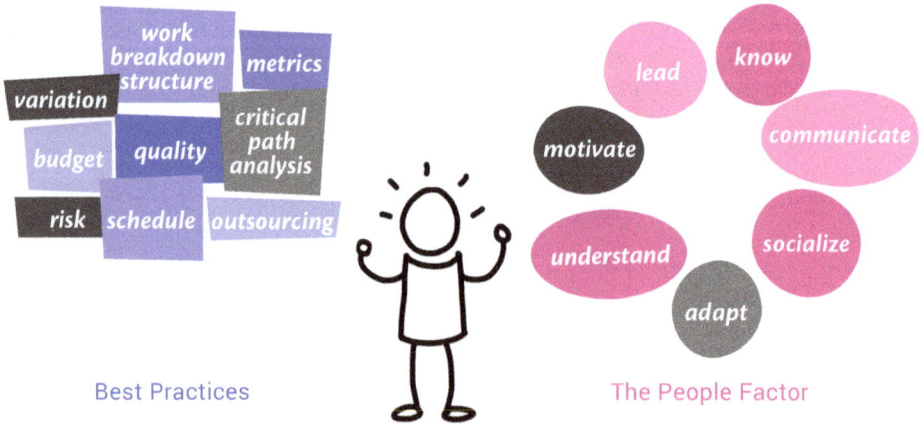

Best Practices   The People Factor

Increase project success!

Before going into the breakdown of the seven skills in the next section, I want to leave you with a final thought. While it might make sense to conclude that the skills of the People Factor are solely directed at project managers, in my view, this is a too narrow view of projects. As I mentioned before, the commitment of everyone involved is what will make a project a success. I collected many examples of how, for instance, a lead engineer coached a junior engineer in a project. Or how socializing between people in projects resulted in a greater feeling of commitment all around, which had a direct, positive influence on the project outcome. The skills of the People Factor are meant for any project professional to develop and put into use, not just the project manager.

"If pressure is on people-focus goes down the drain."
–Eilif Eide, Subsea Engineer, Norway

Key takeaways

- Organizations operate using a combination of business-as-usual and projects.

- Projects are specific endeavors to get things done, contributing to the overall stability and sustainability of an organization.

- Projects are run by cross-functional teams of professionals who are not afraid to take on a challenge.

- Project management best practices are composed of formal, disciplined, purely logical whats and hows.

■ The skills of the People Factor are mission-critical and have a tremendous impact on the outcome of a project.

■ The People Factor's seven-skills framework consists of: know, communicate, socialize, adapt, understand, motivate and lead.

■ Every project professional needs both traditional best practices and the People Factor's skills to influence the successful outcome of projects.

• •

THE PEOPLE FACTOR

Once you unlock the keys to the people in projects, you unlock the keys to project success. People are the backbone, and they are the most valuable resource available to you as a project manager—this is why vital people-related skills like communication, leadership and motivation will help you succeed.

In this second part of the book, you will find a chapter-by-chapter breakdown of the seven skills that make up the People Factor. It bears emphasis again: These skills are critical to project success. They directly influence the establishment of connectivity and commitment amongst the project team, and they guarantee setting the accomplishment of the project goals as the joint priority.

These skills have been defined based on a review of previously conducted research in combination with data from interviews. A group of fifty experienced international project professionals have been interviewed over the course of the last five years, which has enriched the book with real-life examples of how the People Factor's seven skills can be put to use and how they already are being used. Each chapter gives you advice and suggestions on how to develop the specific skill.

Now, let's dig in!

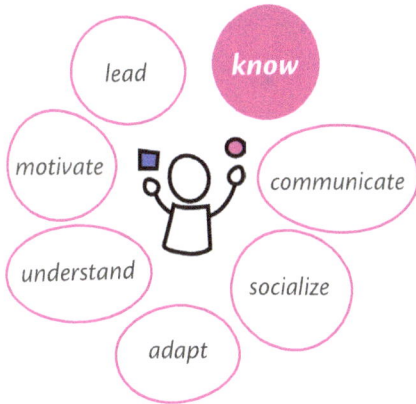

CHAPTER 1

KNOW

In the introduction, I touched upon the nature versus nurture debate of being a successful project manager. I introduced three traits that work well with the job: liking people, dealing with change, and navigating complexity. I see having these traits like Jim Collins's book, Good to Great—without them, you can be a good project manager, but with them, you can be great. Knowing what your natural traits are and deciding what skills you need to develop starts by understanding who you are. In short, you need to know yourself. This is the first aspect of the **know** skill.

"An investment in knowledge always pays the best interest." –Ben Franklin

Know Yourself

The 'self' is a general term used in psychology to refer to how someone thinks about, evaluates and perceives their being. It is the information one draws upon when answering questions like "Who am I?" and "What am I like?" Lewis (1990) suggests that development of the self has two aspects: the existential self, which is the most basic part of the self, referring to the sense of being separate and distinct from others; and the categorical self, which refers to the sense of being an object in the world in connection to others. In Turner's self-categorization theory (1978), the existential self consists of personal identity, which relies on self-evaluation. And the categorical self or social identity relies on how others perceive us. Both parts make up the totality of how we perceive ourselves.

But what do we know when we state we know ourselves? And how do we gain access to this knowledge? According to McAdams (1995), who conducted research in the field of narrative psychology, knowledge of oneself can be categorized into three different levels:

Level 1	Dispositional traits	This level is comprised of broad, general traits and tendencies. A few examples are how shy, outgoing, intelligent or warm someone is.
Level 2	Characteristic adaptations	This level consists of personal concerns, which describe what someone wants and what they want to avoid, as well as what life methods they use to get or avoid these things. Desires, values, beliefs, concerns and coping mechanisms are a few examples of personal concerns.
Level 3	Life stories	This level holds someone's life stories, which make the narratives more alive and real-seeming. According to McAdams. these are the details that give a sense of unity, meaning and purpose to someone's life.

Making use of the three-level model of personality results in a systematic, organized collection of information from which a good description of yourself or others can be made.

Science does not agree on when the development of the self begins. Some researchers say it is as early as three years old, while others say it starts somewhere around seven or eight years of age. One way or another, in pre-adulthood, the self undergoes a significant change, after which the overall self only changes gradually, with existing concepts being redefined and solidified.

Although the explanation of the self sounds pretty simple, it is particularly hard to have certain kinds of insights about oneself. There are some major obstacles to overcome in terms of gaining self-knowledge, which are universal for all humans alike:

- Much of what we do is unconscious. We have evolved into creatures whose minds are divided into conscious and unconscious processes. The reason for this division is bandwidth. It is extremely straining for the brain to stay conscious in every single moment of our feelings, intentions and behaviors; it is a lot easier to live with much of this on auto-pilot.

- According to Freud, there is extraordinary resistance from our part to making a lot of our unconscious material conscious. We might discover, if we get to know ourselves better, that we have desires or ambitions quite different from those our society expects of us. By not going there, we reduce our immediate discomfort; however, this comes at the cost of the opportunity to properly aim for what will truly make us happy.

- It is hard to see by ourselves the many intricate aspects of our identities. We need others to be our mirrors, feeding us back insights and perspectives on the hard-to-see parts of ourselves. However, getting hold of data from others is a very unreliable process. People either tend to dislike us or be neutral about us and thus can't be bothered making the effort, or on the flip side, like us too much and not want to upset us. Receiving reliable feedback can be a daunting task.

- Knowledge of the self can only evolve as a result of experience. It is acquired dynamically, by trying new things and colliding with others, which carries with it risk and takes time. In careers, for example, we can't know what we might want to do with our lives simply by asking ourselves the question. We need to head out into the workplace and try things out.

- Vagueness is a universal problem among humans. The first reports of our conscious minds are by nature horribly vague and not accurate enough to help guide action. "I want to be creative," for instance, or "He annoys me" might be true, but they don't help us get a grip on what is really happening.

Despite these obstacles, I believe everyone can agree on the importance of understanding and developing the self. Armed with self-knowledge, we have a greater chance at happiness, life-satisfaction, positive self-esteem, and achievement. Self-knowledge allows for the correct formulation of our life choices as we understand and can lead ourselves from our intrinsic emotions and preferences. It also allows us to avoid errors in our dealings with others.

As a project manager, you are charged with getting goals met through the efforts of others. Influencing the efforts of others starts by understanding your own role and behavior. For this, you need to know yourself. Let's look at an example:

Your colleague who is a project manager acts like a bully. He's very competent at keeping his projects within budget and delivered on time, but he lacks social skills. He does not listen and gives special treatment to only those people he likes. And he does not like you. One day, you sit down with your team in the lunchroom, where a discussion is ongoing about your colleague. Apparently, you are not the only one having issues with him. One of your team members expresses she does not want to work with him anymore, and that if she is assigned to one of his projects, she will request a formal transfer or ultimately leave the company all-together. You can't blame her; you have experienced the examples she describes of him bullying her in relation to yourself as well. All of it doesn't sound good. You contemplate the new information you've picked up for some days before deciding you are going to give feedback to your colleague on his behavior. You invite him for a meeting and introduce upfront the topic you want to discuss. Within ten minutes, the meeting is over. The conversation did not turn out the way you hoped. Your colleague did not value any of your concerns and did not recognize why any of his behavior could be a contributor. He did not see the feedback as a gift toward self-improvement, but rather as a personal attack on his character.

Having an understanding of yourself allows you to act on your capabilities and be aware of when you might need help or could be wrong. In the example above, your colleague does not have enough knowledge of himself to see that his behavior is affecting situations and people around him. It is not about being wrong or right or finding a common ground on what good and bad behavior is. It is about recognizing that your own tendencies, beliefs or life stories are affecting your behavior. Knowledge of the self lets you understand what your triggers are and gives you an opportunity to adjust how you act. Armed with self-knowledge, you are able to continuously improve your own performance to maximize your positive impact on others.

The model of personality by McAdams only answered what we need to know when we state we know ourselves. The next step is to gain access to this knowledge. Gaining access to the existential self can be done through **Reflection** practices. Access to the categorical self can be obtained through the use of **Feedback** receiving. Let's explore both these techniques.

Gaining knowledge of the existential self means gaining insight into how you perceive yourself and how these insights affect your behavior. You can use what you learn to enhance your life-satisfaction and improve your accomplishments as a project manager. Gaining insight does not mean you are starting a journey to change who you are. Instead, you want to understand better what triggers certain behaviors in yourself and how you can make ever-so-slight changes to enhance your positive impact on others.

One of the most effective means to gain insight into yourself is through reflection practices. The word 'reflect' in Latin means to 'bend back, turn back.' Like the example of your reflection looking back at you in the mirror, looking at events and your own behavior gives you new insights in return. Reflection is looking inward, so you can then look out with a more accurate understanding of yourself, of where you're looking from. The more accurate you are, the closer you get to your true authentic self, which in return gives you greater life-satisfaction and accomplishment.

Taking time to reflect allows you to take notice and become more mindful of what is happening in situations that are influenced by your presence and

behavior. In the best-case scenario, your self is in seamless alignment with your behavior, but this is not the case for most of us. It
is absolutely possible for even the most self-aware person to submit
to a moment of emotional reactivity, yelling or cursing. This kind of
reactive behavior should happen less often, though, as you become
more knowledgeable about your own triggers and more able to
practice self-control. I will come back to the latter and how it relates
to the People Factor in a later chapter.

Reflection is a dynamic process. It is not about being passive,
staying where you are and looking back, but rather it is an active
engagement with knowledge and experience. The reflection model I
use and keep returning to over time is one I received from an executive coach I worked with many years ago. It is simple to use and
comprises the following four steps:

1. **Stop:** Everybody is busy. Life keeps trotting on unless,
   once in a while, you stop. Take a step back from your daily
   activities and think about what you feel about yourself, in
   a certain situation or context, or just in general.

2. **Look:** Once you stop, it is time to look. Look at yourself, your life and your own actions and behavior. Look
   honestly at how they have affected you as a person or the
   situation you are in. Look deeply, not just on a shallow
   level. Explore your life and experiences, and be true to
   yourself.

3. **Listen:** Next, it is time to listen. It can be comforting
   and supportive to get outside guidance and wise coun-
   sel when problems arise, but let's not forget about our
   inner guide. Maslov (1943) and other psychologists say
   that people who are less dependent on others and more
   self-directed in making life decisions tend to have more

positive mental health. Develop a practice of turning inward and listening to your intuitive voice, which knows what it is you really want, what really fits you and gives meaning and direction to life. Mindfulness practices, such as keeping a journal or connection with nature, are examples of tools to strengthen this ability to tap into your inner guidance and wisdom.

4. **Act:** Now that you have stopped, looked and listened, it is time to act. You have new insights and perhaps new steps you want to take to adjust, change or improve. It is time to put these steps into action. Once you have taken action, you might want to return to Step 1. Reflection doesn't have a distinct beginning or end—it can be used continuously throughout the span of your career or life.

There are other frameworks and models to use as well. They all encourage a structured process to guide you. Here are a few examples to consider:

- The reflective cycle by Gibbs (1988), which is based on David Kolb's experiential cycle stages (1984). This is probably the most cited model and suggests a full analysis of a situation by using prompt questions at each stage.

- The model of structured reflection (MSR) by Johns (2006) is based on the patterns of knowing model by Carper (1978). It uses a similar process as the reflective cycle by Gibbs, but adds reflexivity, which is the knowledge of how the experience connects with previous experiences.

- Borton (1970) uses three stem questions to reflect on situations and experiences. By asking ourselves 'What?', 'So what?' and 'Now what?', combined with trigger questions for every stem question, the reflective cycle is completed.

Investigate some of the models or find more, and see what works best for you. There is no one-size-fits-all when it comes to the practice of reflection.

"I interact with myself regularly. It is a great way to reflect on how I am doing and what of myself requires development."
–Mirjam van der Plas, Associate
Director Advisory Group Health, Safety
& Environment, the Netherlands

Gaining knowledge of the categorical self means gaining insights in how others perceive you and how this perception affects your behavior. It could be that your own self-image is not the way others see you. This is actually the most likely case. Through reflection practices, you might have concluded you are a tough but fair person, while others might perceive you to be the opposite. No worries, there is a fix for this, which I will get to later. Firstly, though, you need to gain access to how other people perceive you.

The best way to do this is by actively seeking feedback. Receiving feedback is a great tool when it comes to your personal development. It allows for others to make transparent if something in your behavior is disagreeable. This can then help you make changes if you want to, which is a crucial step of this feedback, as it makes the activity constructive instead of degrading.

Opening yourself up and asking for feedback can be daunting. The uncertainty of someone's intentions or the fear of a personal attack can be hard to handle. However, your willingness and ability to receive feedback mean you get another step closer to an accurate understanding of yourself, which in return gives you a greater sense of well-being and accomplishment. When asking for feedback, keep in mind the following:

Identify the right feedback givers

The best place to start is with your closest circle. Think of your partner, your family or friend(s). Anyone who is close to you should be able to give you insight into your strengths and the things you could do better. Once you've asked your close circle, consider widening your search. Think of people you might have worked closely with on a certain project or your peers in general. Feedback from different sources gives you more perspective and helps you form a more complete view of yourself. Keep in mind, though, that you want to gain insights into how others perceive you as a person broadly, not only in terms of your professional role.

Prepare what you want to receive feedback on

Asking someone what they think about you as a general question usually does not lead to constructive feedback. Ask specific questions related to topics you want to know more about. These can be yes/no questions to confirm or deny a thought you have about yourself. They can also be open-ended questions that will give you additional information about a certain topic. Example questions are:

✓ What do you think are my strengths?

✓ If you were to give me one insight about my behavior
   that you think I am unaware of, what would it be?

✓ What could I do to improve a negative behavior of mine?

✓ What do you think are my weaknesses?

It might also help the feedback-givers to receive your questions upfront. This allows them to understand what you want to know and prepare in advance as opposed to being caught off-guard, which can make the feedback activity more effective and enjoyable for you both.

Make sure your energy levels are up

Asking questions and hearing answers about how other people perceive you is not easy (unless, of course, it only includes compliments). Everyone holds a few criticisms about each person they know, even those they love the most. Make sure you have gotten enough sleep and are energized before receiving feedback. It is better to reschedule than to end up in a fight because you have difficulties controlling your emotions and thoughts.

You are now ready to sit down with someone. You are energized and have your questions ready. Generally, the process you are about to experience will take you through three different stages once you've heard their feedback. You will react, you will reflect, and you will respond. The tips on the next page provide guidance on each of these stages:

React	During this stage, you: • Need to be aware of and manage your emotional reaction to what you are hearing. • Should concentrate on listening to the feedback and ask questions to ensure you understand the other person's views. • Must remember not to skip to the last stage and respond. Depending on what the feedback is, you might need to end the conversation early to give yourself time to think properly about what you have heard.
Reflect	During this stage, you: • Should be honest with yourself and open about what the other person said. • Should allow yourself extra time for your emotions to calm down if needed. • Ask for specific examples to help you understand the feedback if required.
Respond	During this stage, you: • Accept the feedback by thanking the feedback-giver. • Can respectfully say so if you don't agree with the feedback. Don't argue with the feedback-giver, though! You can also choose not to respond. • Should focus on the future. You have just received valuable insights into how another person perceives you, and this makes you more knowledgeable about yourself. • Can, if you feel like an improvement of your behavior is needed, solicit options or solutions and discuss potential next steps.

Through receiving feedback, you gain great insights into how others perceive you. It may end up that this is not aligned with the way you see yourself. A reason for this could be your own unintentional bias or inaccurate judgment of others toward you. However, you might want to consider as well how much of your personality you make visible to others. If you don't open up to the people around you, they tend to project a wealth of assumptions onto you. You have no control over if these assumptions will work for you or not. Promoting the strengths and qualities you have is a good way to reinforce the way you want to be perceived. For this to work, you need to intentionally make information about yourself available to others, information that should provide evidence of the strengths and qualities you are trying to reveal. If others see you the way you see yourself, life is simply easier and more rewarding. You get opportunities and support that are a good fit for you, which pays off in life-satisfaction and accomplishment.

One of the project professionals I talked to gave me the following example when talking about feedback and reflection:

"The company I work with is trying to develop a culture of continuous feedback amongst employees. It started a while ago. They encourage people to give feedback to each other. They introduced a software tool for feedback many years ago and now, little by little, it's being promoted to use on a more regular basis than only once a year.

I asked two of my peers to give me feedback. Some things where quite obvious to me, while others made me think. Both of them said independently of each other that I should make more time for myself and my family. I reflected on this for a while and started keeping track of how much time I actually spent at work or connected to work. I became more aware of the effect it had on me and my family when I opened my laptop for the sixth time over the course of a weekend. I always believed this was needed to stay on top of things and not have issues stacking up to a point where I could not handle them anymore.

It took me some months before I was able to not look at my phone regularly in the evening and the weekend to finally shutting it down on occasion as well. I feel much more energized and ready for the week now, while I think I was getting dangerously close to a burnout before. Receiving feedback turned out to be a valuable practice in my self-development."

Throughout the practice of knowing yourself, keep a journal to write down the insights you gain through self-reflection and receiving feedback. See if you can uncover patterns in your behavior that work counterproductive to what you are trying to achieve. Bit by bit, you will get a fuller picture of who you are and what you are like, as well as what your impact is on the people around you. See each discovery you make as a gift toward living an authentic and fuller life.

"I know perhaps I am not so good at self-awareness, but I have the willingness to do better."
—Yannick Avril, Director of Engineering
& Construction for Asia Pacific, China

One of the project professionals I interviewed mentioned the following example of reflection practices:

*"I have the **Management Tips: From Harvard Business Review** book in the top drawer of my desk. Each morning when I arrive at the office, I read a tip from one of its*

pages. The tip is not always specifically related to what I am busy with that day, but I try to think about it a couple of times a day to see how it could help. They include, for instance: 'Be open to criticism,' or 'Schedule regular meetings with yourself.' When I arrive at the office the next day, I take out the book again. Before picking a new tip for that day, I reflect on how the tip from the previous day worked for me. Was it useful? What was the effect? Can I make it part of my skillset? And so on. After I am done reflecting, I pick a new tip from the book for the new day. I have been doing this for some while now. It has really helped me understand some of my own behavior and what its effect is on the people around me. I can highly recommend it to anyone who wants to continuously learn and improve.'

Know Others

In the perfect project world, everyone has an adequate understanding of themselves and acts in ways that support the project goals. Their individual and varied interests, desires, and traits work well together and make up for a strong team. Sounds like a fantasy, right? Well, it is. Real life is unpredictable, and human behavior is fickle. As a project manager, you need to work with the temperaments, wants, and narratives of each individual in the project team to achieve the project goal. This is daunting.

Knowing yourself isn't much different from knowing others. Everyone has their own personal traits, desires, and life stories that predict the preferences they have and how they behave. It is for you to find out what these are so you can adjust your own behavior and approach toward each individual. Additionally, knowing others individually is an important skill to understand how people behave and interact within a group. This is called team dynamics. These aspects of knowing others are the second aspect of **know**.

There are some tools you can use to get to know the people in your project organization better. Using the three levels of personality by McAdams (1995), you want to know more about someone's dispositional traits, characteristic adaptations, and life stories. To gain insight into the first two levels, you could make use of the following:

- The Myers-Briggs Type Indicator (MBTI) is a questionnaire based on work by psychiatrist Carl Jung, who thought that people understood the world through four functions: sensation, intuition, feeling, and thinking. It emphasizes the value of naturally occurring differences in people and assumes that everyone has specific preferences originating from individual interest, values, and needs. It is a very popular model in the business world and is used on a regular basis in assessments of individuals and teams.

- The DISC profile, a tool based on the ideas of psychologists W. Marston and W. Clarke, measures someone's preferences and tendencies and categorizes them using four basic behavior styles: dominance, influence, steadiness, and conscientiousness. It is an easy-to-use tool that is practiced in combinations of theory and

games in many development programs. I have used the
DISC tool myself on occasion as well, in both projects and
workshops. It has a low threshold and is easily accessible.

- The Big Five personality traits, also known as the five-
  factor model or the OCEAN model, uses five factors to
  depict the human personality. These factors are: openness, conscientiousness, extraversion, agreeableness,
  and neuroticism. This is based on the assumption that if
  personality characteristics are the most important aspect
  of people's lives, they will become part of their language.

It is not uncommon for the human resource department of
your company to have outcomes of personality tests available for
all employees. Perhaps you can get access to them to make a good
assessment of the team. If not, or if you want to include the external
team as well, see if you have some freedom to be creative with the
topic in the kick-off meeting of the project. There are fun games out
there that you can use to gather the information you need about
the people you are working with. Using a team-building activity is a
great way of getting to know more about their individual narratives
as well. Try to incorporate elements of storytelling or working with
visualizations of life stories. Be creative. And always keep in mind
that the more you know about someone, the easier it is to work
together toward reaching the project goal.

Knowing the individual personalities of
your project team still does not make
for a strong team on its own. It is the
project manager's responsibility to
create and reinforce an environment
in which the right behavior flourishes,
and the wrong behavior dies. This is all

to ensure the project team, which is a living, constantly changing, dynamic force, remains committed to the successful joint completion of the project.

In 1965, B.W. Tuckman created a model to describe the behaviors and interactions of people during various phases of team development. His well-known model, which consists of five stages, became a benchmark for team development. The five stages and what is expected of you as the project manager are as follows:

1. ***Forming***

In the forming stage, people look to the group leader for guidance and direction. In the project environment, this leader would be you as the project manager. In this stage, everyone will have a desire to better understand the scope of the project and how to approach it (and each other). Try to keep this stage simple, and try to go through it quick. You don't want the team to get stuck in a web of politeness and political correctness, unwilling to address concerns. For the team to mature, they need to be ready for what is to come.

2. ***Storming***

The second stage of team development is often less pleasant, characterized by competition and conflict. Team members have to mold their feelings, ideas, and beliefs to suit the group, which results in questions to contest roles, accountabilities, and rank. In order to progress to the next stage of team development, the group needs to move from a testing mentality to one of problem-solving. As a project manager, it is important to take control of the group and provide clear direction and guidance to help this progress.

3. *Norming*

During the norming stage, the rules of the game are established. Team members need to let go of preconceived ideas or opinions and actively acknowledge the contributions of everyone in the team. Cliques need to dissolve for team cohesion to emerge. This is a difficult phase for many, as they need to adhere to a certain structure and obligations that might feel like an infringement on individual rights and liberties. Many teams fail during this complex period of norming. As a project manager, you need to make sure this stage remains simple and goes quickly. Don't spent too much time on establishing rules and getting everyone on board. Before you know it, everyone will already be on their way to the next project. Establish a minimal framework that everyone can agree and adhere too.

4. *Performing*

Tuckman observed that high-performance teams only emerge after having gone through the forming, storming, and norming stages. Many teams, however, never reach this point. In this stage, people can absorb blows, have no need for personal egos, and are connected by a powerful shared purpose. They can work individually, in subgroups or as a total unit, in which roles and authorities dynamically adjust to the changing needs of the group or individual. People trust one another with their ups and downs and hold each other accountable for selfish behavior. As a project manager, you try to influence your team's maturity in this stage by setting the example of the behavior you wish them to display. Your own vulnerability plays a vital role in this.

5. *Adjourning*

The final stage, adjourning, involves the termination of tasks and the disengagement of relationships. It includes recognition for participation and an opportunity to say personal goodbyes. As a project manager, it is important for you to facilitate this ending of the project to celebrate the ever-increasing network of acquaintances and friends that have been created along the way.

Knowing the development process of teams is not enough on its own to create and reinforce an environment in which the right behavior flourishes and the wrong behavior dies. To accomplish this, you need to facilitate giving and receiving of feedback amongst the team. Feedback is one of the best tools when it comes to personal development and the progression of a group. Feedback means giving and getting both praise and criticism. It is about making transparent that there is something in a person's behavior that is disagreeable and helping that person to adjust that behavioral element. The latter is crucial in feedback, as it makes the activity constructive instead of degrading.

There are a number of important factors to keep in mind when facilitating giving and receiving of feedback.

- Create safety. If the receiver of the feedback doesn't feel comfortable, the feedback will reach deaf ears. Adding civility and safety into the feedback approach results in a more productive and applied feedback. Consider the following approaches:

  ✓ Earn and extend trust. Encourage honesty amongst the team by admitting when you don't know something. Following through on your word, explaining yourself, and including others are all practical ways to build trust amongst the team.

  ✓ Find out how the team likes to receive feedback. Take the time to ask them upfront what they prefer regarding things like communication styles and types of feedback.

✓ Welcome curiosity. Follow the path the team takes you on in discovering how giving and receiving of feedback works. The approaches in this book are guidelines to get you going rather than rules to live by. Experiment, and be creative in what works.

- Ensure feedback is given on someone's behavior, not their personality or character. The purpose of giving feedback is not to change someone, it is to adjust specific behavior. "You are rude" or "You are inconsiderate," for example, are directed at someone's character, not their behavior. The key problem with this kind of feedback is that it is someone's interpretation, which could be perceived as insulting. You don't want the team to end up in an argument over someone's personality instead of how they behave.

- When feedback is given, try to ensure it is as specific as possible. There is no value, for instance, in telling a team member they need to work better with colleagues without giving specific examples to describe why this is the case. By giving examples, you give the receiver a much better chance of improving their behavior. A great model to influence being specific is the STAR model, which stands for Situation, Task, Action and Result. In the table on the next page, I provide examples of giving feedback according to the STAR model.

Situation Describe the situation – What? When? Who?	"I felt you really supported me when I missed the deadline Friday."	"I've noticed that you came in to work at 9:30 a.m. three times this week."
Task What is expected in relation to work, behavior, or tasks?	"I had expected you to be really frustrated, because we had committed to it, but . . ."	"Your shift starts at 8 a.m. It's in our team agreement that we are all on time in the morning."
Action How did what happened meet or fall short of those expectations?	"You understood and told everyone that it wasn't my fault."	"Because you came into work later, it meant that someone else had to take over your work until you came in."
Result The outcome or impact of the action.	"So I'd like to say thanks, I feel much better about things."	"It was extremely busy, and being 'one person down' put a lot of unnecessary pressure on the rest of the team."

Firstly, having knowledge of the individuals in your project team is a great way to start when dealing with individual temperaments, wants, and narratives. Having knowledge of the process your project team will go through when developing into a high-performing team is a great way to influence their maturity. And finally, having the knowledge to facilitate feedback within your team will set you and the team up to achieve the project goal. If this, however, still isn't enough to ensure high performance, you might want to consider coaching the team as well.

One of the project professionals I spoke to gave me the following example related to knowing others:

"I used to work in a company where, as a project manager, you had a say in whom you wanted to work with in your projects. Most of my colleagues preferred to work with the high-performing team members. However, there was also one colleague that used to go for the ones who were not so sought-after. He wanted to make sure he was able to lead and organize without too much conflict in the team and choose the team based on this.

After establishing the team, he was able to detect the strengths and weaknesses of everyone very quickly and organize them in such a way that they functioned well together. He made time to develop and support team members who needed help, and in this way was able to maintain great results in his projects."

"Coaching is unlocking a person's potential to maximize their own performance."
–Sir John Whitmore

Coaching is about helping team members discover their own potential without directly telling them what to do or think. It is about unlocking the potential that is already there by removing barriers that might exist, often ones created by the people themselves.

Coaching can occur at any time or place and can be a great motivator. Knowing that you are there to help them can make the difference between good and great performance. Just look at some of the top sportspeople in the world. They all have coaches who help them achieve extraordinary results.

Before starting to coach people in your team, there are some minimum requirements to keep in mind, including the following:

- Before coaching anyone, make sure you have the ability to coach. There's lots of curriculum available these days to help you pick up coaching skills. Make sure you have these skills before practicing coaching with your team.

- Before you start coaching, first check if the individual or team is willing to be coached. Although there currently is a lot of hype surrounding coaching, there still remains a significant likelihood that someone will not be interested. Be respectful of someone's choices before putting your hard-earned skills to the test.

- Coaching is a collaborative effort between two or more people in which a relationship is established. Like in any relationship, its value relies on the establishment of trust. Trust is developed by being open, honest, respectful, and considerate, which starts with you setting the example.

- A common mistake people make when coaching is giving advice/direct instruction. This is not the purpose of coaching, though. It is about letting someone else figure out what works for them instead of you telling them what works for you. You might want to consider mentoring or peer-group learning as a better tool to help the development of your team if you find it hard to refrain from giving your opinion.

If you find a team member or the team willing to be coached, you will have to schedule coaching conversations. During these conversations you want to guide them into reflecting and reframing on difficult situations. Often this will be situations related to work-life, but don't be surprised if private situations come up also. There are a couple of behaviors you want to consider during the conversations that will help you guide their development:

- Be curious, and ask a lot of questions. Curiosity builds trust by showing interest in what is going on with the team member or group. To be truly curious means to set aside your own ideas and opinions. Don't interrupt, but do try to paraphrase the key elements you hear back to them. To get someone or the team talking, ask open-ended questions that start with 'what' and 'how.' Try to avoid 'why' questions, as they can make a person defensive. Some questions that could help you get started are:

  ✓ What is on your mind?

  ✓ What is the real challenge for you?

  ✓ What do you want?

  ✓ How can I help?

- Focus on the team member or group. You want to meet in a place that is quiet and without distractions. Make sure phones are turned off and laptops closed. This includes yours as well.

- Try to be empathetic about what the team member or group is feeling. When you understand and acknowledge where they are coming from, you come across as trustworthy and relatable. Ask yourself why someone is feeling this way, and what you can do to help.

"Talent wins games, but teamwork wins championships."
—Michael Jordan

One of the project professionals I interviewed provided the following insight about the project team:

"When I was young, I was a football player. I see the project team in the same way as I see a soccer team. We all have one objective. But when we are in the field, we do not only have one role. If someone is having difficulties, we need to compensate. This only happens when there is trust amongst the team and they are willing to support each other. If people are only focused on their job and don't care about what is going on around them, this is catastrophic.

I promote trust by being transparent, by sharing information. I do so as much as possible in meetings and individually. I listen and make an effort to understand and acknowledge challenges and difficulties. This is, for me, the way to promote trust and support amongst the team."

Key takeaways

- Unlocking your true potential starts by knowing yourself.

- Reflection and feedback practices get you closer to know-ing your true self.

- Knowing others helps you deal with differences in person-ality and behavior.

- Making time to know, guide, and coach the project team will influence their maturity, resulting in higher performance.

- Know that you can always expand upon your knowing.

COMMUNICATE

lead

know

motivate

communicate

understand

socialize

adapt

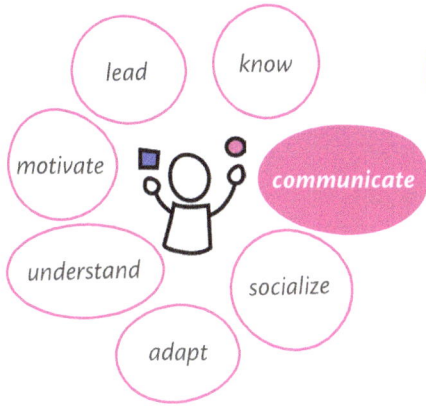

Wherever there are people, there is communication. Whatever they do and with whom, how, and why they do it, they communicate. Whatever they want to achieve, they need communication for it. We are a communicative species. We use communication when we talk, listen, write, or read. **Communicate** is the second skill of the People Factor.

"You can change your world by changing your words."
—Joel Osteen

Communication occurs when a person expresses an emotion, feeling, thought, or idea, or senses the need to communicate. The communication process is triggered when the sender makes a conscious or unconscious decision to share a message with another person, the receiver. When the receiver gets the message, they will usually give feedback (a return message) unconsciously or consciously. Thus, the communication process is always on-going.

Every act of communication is based on something that conveys meaning, and that conveyance is the message. This message can be either verbal (spoken or written) or nonverbal (body language, physical appearance, or vocal tone). The message can be received by either listening, receiving, or observing.

Every message is sent and received through one of our five senses. It is seen, heard, touched, tasted, or smelled. These sensory media through which messages are sent and received are communication channels. Messages might be seen through body movement, letters, memos, instant messaging, signs, emails, and so on. Messages that are heard come through conversations, presentations, telephone calls, radio, and other audio media. Sight- and sound-based media are the two most frequently used communication methods in the world today.

The communication process consists of three main elements: sending a message, receiving a message, and interpreting the message.

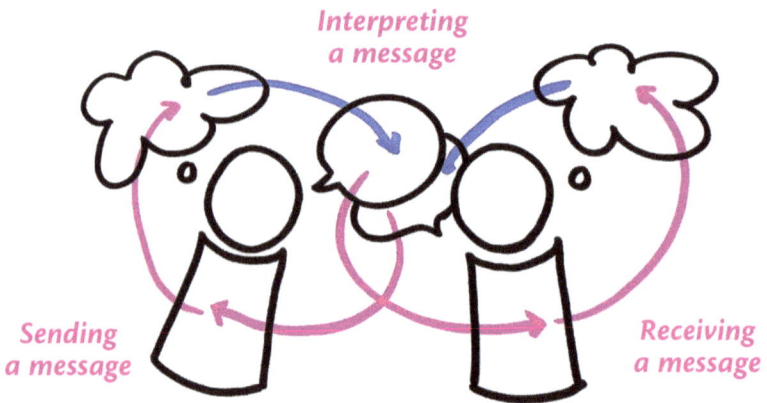

Interpreting a message

Sending a message

Receiving a message

Sending a message involves verbal and non-verbal communication. Verbal communication means sharing a message using speech or writing. It encompasses everything from simple one-syllable sounds and words to complex discussions, and relies on both language and emotion to produce the desired effect. Although all species communicate, language itself is an exclusively human property. Today, about 6,900 languages are spoken throughout the world. They can be grouped into more than 90 language families, all of which have a common origin. Science is not unified about when and where this language originated from.

Through non-verbal communication, people show their intentions and feelings, whether they are aware of it or not. They can become unintentional senders of subtle messages about what is actually going on inside. Research shows that over half of the meaning that others attach to spoken messages comes not from the wording of the message itself, but from the tone of voice and body language. This nonverbal impact comes particularly from the face, eyes, body, clothing, and gestures, as well as touch. Usually, it comes in a package of multiple signals at once.

Although the verbal- and non-verbal aspects of our messages are often consistent, they can also be out of line with each other. If someone's words conflict with, for instance, their tone of voice, we often mistrust the words and believe the non-verbal clues instead. It is not very convincing, for example, when someone tells you they're not angry at you, while avoiding looking at you and wearing an angry expression on their face.

> The following is an example from my own career. It is not specifically related to projects, but it should give you an idea of the presence and importance of body language:
>
> *In 2017, I started a year-long post-bachelor professional trainer course in which I gained insights on didactic models and tools and developed skills to effectively train project professionals. As part of the final exam, I needed to find a company willing to facilitate a full-day training on a development topic within their organization or team. Together*

with a classmate, I found a branch of the Dutch tax office prepared to host our exam. During the day, we would be taped, allowing the instructor of the course to grade us.

We worked long and hard on finding a good development topic for the team. We made a program for the day, including a presentation, exercises, and even a card game. We divided the program into various pieces and allocated out the workload. I ended up with the presentation part to kick off the morning. While making the presentation, I was unsure about a certain part of the content. I anticipated someone smart could ask me a question that would not be easy to answer. I decided to leave that part in the presentation and see how it would play out—I did not mitigate the risk. I did a couple of test-runs before the exam day, and no one asked me anything about it. I felt confident in going for it. Three minutes into my presentation, I got the one shitty question I was trying to avoid.

A couple of weeks later, I had to appear in front of the examination committee to defend my work during the year, including the training at the tax office. One of the comments I got was that although I did not evade answering the difficult question and the answer was pretty good, my body language spoke irritation. My overall grade had been lowered due to this.

Receiving a message can mean making use of both listening and reading, which are part of verbal communication, and observing, which is part of non-verbal communication.

Listening involves active participation in the conversation. Effective listeners actually hear what is said rather than assuming. They question and reflect, which demonstrates that they are both listening and interested. Passive listeners are attentive but do nothing to assist the sender. Because there is a difference in how fast someone can speak and how fast others can listen, a time lag exists in conversations. Effective listeners do not daydream during this lag; they use the time to reflect on what has been said and to question and clarify parts of the message that are not clear.

"When a room is relaxed, people tend to lean back in their chairs. When the opposite is the case, people tend to have their arms crossed, with elbows in position, ready to fight. Watching body language has really helped me in meetings in terms of getting my message across."
—Tish Layton, Associate Director: Project Controls, US

By observing, you also receive non-verbal messages. The sender's mannerisms, accent, dress, or grooming can convey something different than the actual words used. People who are better readers of nonverbal messages tend to look at the totality of these cues rather than isolating them.

On a daily basis, we spend a substantial amount of time receiving written messages as well. Instant messages, emails, manuals, newspapers, online articles, books, magazines, social media posts, and so on—they all involve the ability to read and receive. Most of us learn to read when we are young. However, being an effective reader involves practice. The three most common techniques for effective reading are as follows:

- Skimming: reading rapidly for the main points;

- Scanning: reading rapidly to find a specific piece of information, and;

- Intensive reading: reading a short text carefully for detailed information.

Interpreting involves decoding a message. Decoding happens in a person's mind, and no two minds are the same. Each person's brain will filter and sometimes distort information based on their individual reality. The main communication obstacles leading to wrong interpretation of messages can be narrowed down to the following three categories:

1. Linguistic: Language in itself is an obstacle to communication. How well we master a certain language is an important indicator for how well we will understand the intent of a message. But also, how language is processed

and stored in the brain is different for each person, and remains largely a mystery.

2. Cultural: Culture is essentially the totality of assumptions and values of an individual or group—their perceived reality. Culture is a big contributor to misinterpretation when sending or receiving a message.

3. Political: Wherever and whenever there are many individuals and groups involved, there is the possibility of vested interests and power games getting in the way of communication.

One of the project professionals I interviewed gave me the following example when talking about linguistic communication errors:

"I was working on a project in a hub, which consisted of people from many different cultures and backgrounds. Twenty percent were expats flying into the hub on a weekly basis. The other 80 percent were natives from the country the project was being executed in. One of the things I noticed was that we were all saying the same thing, but we were bringing these terminologies from other projects and other cultures to this project. The gap between old terminology and silly cultural words made for ineffective communication. For example, when a person from the UK says, 'Let's table it,' they want to talk about it right then and there. When a person from the States says the exact same thing, they mean that they don't want to talk about it right now, they want to put it aside and talk about it

later. The group kept saying 'let's table it, let's table it,' and we just kept talking in circles. It's these weird sayings that mean one thing in one country and something else in another. It is interesting to see these things happening. There was something in the way of us communicating, and it was the linguistic part of the communication. So we decided on making a standard dictionary to share among the project to avoid mishaps like this in the future. It was the easiest solution, and it made a big impact right away."

Other factors that influence the interpretation of a message are time and place or context, as well as the well-being of the sender and receiver. How a disagreement is settled, for instance, is highly influenced by where the conversation takes place, as well as how the participants in the conversation are feeling. People who are feeling unwell physically or emotionally tend to focus on the negative aspects and could miss out on the actual intent of the message.

Aside from personal communication, which is used on a daily basis to interact with family and friends, there is also professional communication. Professional communication is an essential part of a workplace and is gaining in importance every day. This is the case in project management. The Project Management Institute (PMI) calls communication the 'life-blood' of each project. Communication is part of every step of the project lifecycle and an essential skill for each project manager to master.

To be able to grasp the full scope of communication in projects, it is important to be aware of the different communication interfaces you as project manager encounter on a daily basis. There is ongoing communication between yourself and other organizations, such as suppliers or the client. These interfaces are part of the external information exchange. There is also ongoing communication between yourself and various departments within the organization, for instance with the sales & marketing team or with the IT department. Communication between yourself and the project team consists of addressing various disciplines like engineering, quality, cost control, and so on. You also might communicate with distributed teams, where one part of the team resides, for example, in Germany and another part in India. These interfaces are all part of the internal information exchange. You are responsible for making communication work for you within the entire project organization, ensuring the methods used contribute to the goal(s) of the project.

For this you can make use of either active or passive communication methods. An active communication method is used to communicate in the here and now. Examples include face-to-face meetings, video- or telephone-conferencing, and webinars. Passive communication methods are those that allow recipients to respond in their own time, for example email, instant messaging, website-based communication, or project newsletters. Mixing active and passive methods of communication is most effective.

"When you communicate externally you are an ambassador for the company you are representing. How you communicate outside is what sets the standard for how people view you inside."
—Philip Morgan, Project Buyer, Germany

In my own experience as a project manager, I find it difficult to recall a scenario in which I did not use communication in one form or another in my day-to-day job. From sending emails to the client, to speaking with a mechanic in the workshop, to sending out a weekly report to the project director—everything involves communication. I therefore agree with the PMI that communication is of extreme importance in projects.

As you are currently reading my book, I'm going to assume you have a good level of competence when it comes to both sending and receiving messages. However, there are still some important tips on these elements to keep in mind.

When you **speak,** it is important to pay attention. Not just to your own words, but also to how the overall conversation is proceeding. This will help you convey your message more effectively. Also keep in mind the following when using speech as the message medium:

- Just as you expect someone to be an active listener, so should you be an active speaker. Maintain appropriate eye contact and look for body signals to indicate that others are engaged. Remember the example of my exam on the previous pages? Your body language sometimes says more about your intent than you are aware of or able to convey through the words you speak.

- If the other person seems to be disengaged or not listening, pause to inquire if you are making sense. When doing so, ask open-ended questions instead of questions that can only be answered with yes or no. This will allow you to check if the other person is picking up on the message you want to convey, and what their perspective on this is. Some examples of open-ended questions are:

- ✓ What would you like to talk about?

- ✓ Tell me, what's bothering you?

- ✓ So, what's going on?

- ✓ What's been happening since we last met?

- ✓ What makes you think it may be time for a change?

- ✓ What happens when you do that?

- ✓ Such as?

- If you want to make it easier for the other person to pick up your message, it is best to avoid monologues. Stick to the point, and avoid overly lengthy or repetitive statements. It is common to start repeating when we feel like we have not been understood. Instead, pause and leave a period of silence for your words to be digested.

When you **listen** to a team member or the client, make sure you are engaged and active. Sit or stand alertly, and maintain appropriate eye contact. This will help you pick up not only the words, but also the non-verbal clues you need in order to decode the message. Also keep in mind the following when you are on the receiving end of a message:

- It sounds simple, but pay attention. If you are occupied by the report you still need to make or what your rebuttal might be, you will for sure miss out on parts of the message. Research by Bradley (1981) shows that we have the capacity to understand 300 words per minute, but the average speaker only sends 100 to 140 words per minute. The temptation to fill the residual capacity with thoughts is very tempting.

- Show that you are listening by using your own body language. Try nodding occasionally, make use of facial expressions, and maintain an open and interested posture.

- Try to not interrupt the speaker. Allow them to finish each point before asking any questions. Interrupting with counterarguments might lead to frustration, limiting your full understanding of the message.

One of the project professionals I interviewed gave me the following example in relation to understanding of the message:

"I learned over time that there are many cases where you communicate something and believe it is very clear, that it is impossible to be misunderstood, and yet it is almost a guarantee that it is being misunderstood by someone. The example I have in mind is not related to project management as such, but it demonstrates what I mean:

At the beginning of the year, we, the management team, set up initiatives for leadership to use as guidelines when establishing goals and objectives for the year amongst their departments. To us, this was the smartest way, as it would immediately involve all employees. Some months later, during a quarterly strategy meeting between the management team and all supervisors, the question was raised of when the objectives for the year would be available. This baffled us. The objectives had been communicated at the beginning of the year through the initiatives already, and everyone should have been clear about what to do. During the discussion that followed, it became clear that the supervisors were expecting to get a KPI dashboard, the same as they had received every year. We'd forgotten to make sure the supervisors understood what the intention of the initiatives was and what the expectations for them were. It was dramatic to only uncover this several months into the year.

Since this happened, I put a lot more loops into my communication—checkpoints, if you will. I talk to people regularly to check if what I communicated has been understood. If not, I adjust the communication channel I use or the style to approach them with. I made it a practice to verify if my intent is understood and clear before disengaging from the interaction.'

Email is one of the most common and frequent methods of written communication in the workplace, and its use continues to expand. Although emailing can be an easy and effective way to deliver information to others, there is a higher risk of messages becoming 'lost in translation.' The lack of non-verbal clues makes it very difficult to give meaning to the message. Keep in mind the following when using email as the message channel:

- Try to envision the perspective of the recipient. Try to imagine how they will perceive the message before pressing send. It is much easier to be harsh or direct to someone online than in person. Therefore ask yourself if you would have the courage to say the same things face-to-face before sending the email.

- We are less able to think clearly and act appropriately when we are overcome with emotions. Therefore, do not sent an email if you are angry or sad. You can instead write the email and save it as a draft. Once your emotions are settled, you will be in a much better state to evaluate the message and edit it if necessary.

- It is important to know the limits of written humor. The recipient of an email can't see your grin or hear your laugh when you mean something to be funny. Adding emoticons is a potential solution (if that kind of informal communication is appropriate in your profession or industry).

- Last but not least, make a habit of typing your own email address into the recipient box first when you've finished your entire email and are ready to send. It has happened to me several times that I accidentally pressed send on an email full of spelling errors and inconsistencies. Instead of having to follow up your email with an apology, or even worse, a recall, it will just end up in your own mailbox instead, where you can review it before sending it out for real.

Aside from the higher risk of your intended message getting lost in translation, using email as the only form of communication is not advisable. As I mentioned before, it is most effective to mix both active and passive methods of communication. This has been emphasized by many of the project professionals I interviewed for this book. One of them said the following:

> "An effective project manager uses both telephone and face-to-face meetings enhanced with email to communicate with the customer. After a connection through active communication has been established, it is easier to align on things through email. One of the project coordinators I supervised some years ago used only email to communicate with the customer on a project we were on. After a while, I received feedback from the customer that he felt the coordinator was spamming him with emails. He said, 'If he would just come by for a meeting every now and then, we could cover a lot of the questions at the same time, saving me the effort to have to respond to all the emails.' I introduced the practice of on-site meetings as a result. The contact with the customer improved, and the project was completed successfully."

When sending a message, the worst mistake a sender can make is the **assumption** that the message will be received as intended. So many things can go wrong during the communication process that it is far more likely for the message to be misunderstood. The best representation I have ever seen of how the communication process can go wrong is a comic of a tree and a swing. I saw it for the very first time I think perhaps ten years ago, and it has crossed my path several times since in workshops and online. My own representation of this comic is shown on the next page. From my own experience, I can assure you that this representation is often not far off from reality in many projects.

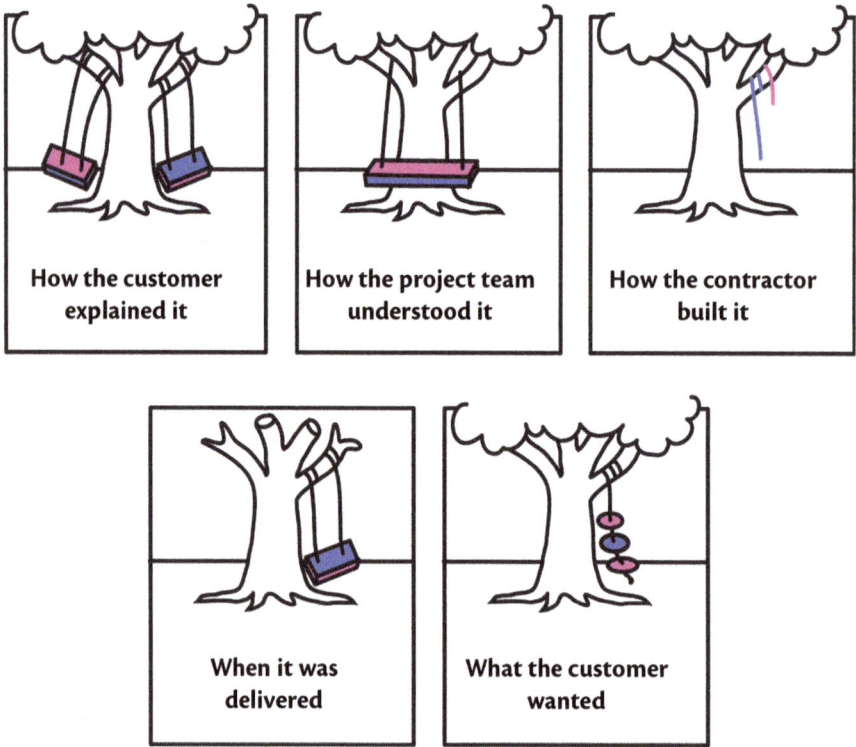

How the customer explained it

How the project team understood it

How the contractor built it

When it was delivered

What the customer wanted

"The single biggest problem in communication is the illusion it has taken place."
—George Bernard Shaw

Obstacles to good communication are always present. We touched upon the three broad areas in this chapter already: linguistic, cultural, and political. The process of overcoming these obstacles starts with awareness that they exist. Being able to spot them in action is not easy—it takes a lot of practice. But being able to take actions to avoid these barriers in your daily communication means you have come one step closer to effectively reaching the project goals. When looking at developing the competency to avoid communication obstacles, keep the following in mind:

1. Linguistics in projects is understood in the sense of specialized terminology used by different disciplines. Schedulers, for example, use terminology such as 'the baseline,' or 'lags.' As a project manager, you need to make an effort to understand the different jargon used by the various disciplines, either through study or experience. You will be able to effectively decode messages yourself and also facilitate, if needed, the correct interpretation of communication between the various interfaces. One of the project professionals I interviewed shared with me the following example of the misuse of project terminology:

"I was talking to my project sponsor. We needed to establish a reporting tool toward senior management, and it had to include metrics. I am used to the term metrics when talking about statistics, while he was more familiar with KPI's. Both have an interchangeable meaning, which we were unaware of at the time. The first twenty minutes of the meeting, we kept going around in circles, trying to convince one another of what we needed. Finally, we had a breakthrough when I decided to walk up to a board to show him a metrics table I had done on another project. It was like watching the light go on. In the next ten minutes, we decided on what metrics to include in the report and I went on to my daily business."

   A great way to overcome jargon obstacles is to introduce a glossary of terminology in your project organization.

2. Communication at the interface between two individuals or organizations with vastly different cultures is difficult. For example, communication between a conservative, risk-averse client and a forward-looking, can-do supplier

can lead to a challenging joint project-planning session. As a project manager, you should facilitate communication by being aware of the differences. In geographically distributed teams, regional culture can come into play as well. It could manifest in differences in fluency of language or social behavior. It is, again, the responsibility of the project manager to be aware of the differences and guide communication toward the project goal.

3. As a project manager, it is important to be aware of the key political players within the internal and external organization. Try to identify them early on and gain confidence and buy-in. This helps eliminate political barriers to project communications.

When using speech or writing, it is important to understand that everyone has a preferred communication style. You have one, as does every person around you. You need to be aware of what your own preferred style is and detect the communication style of the person you are communicating with. Based on this information and situational needs, you can then adjust appropriately.

Research shows there are four main communication styles:

- <u>Assertive</u> communication involves expressing your own needs, desires, ideas, and feelings, while also considering and respecting the needs, desires, ideas, and feelings of others. Assertive communication is open, straightforward, and sincere. The message is clear and does not have any underlying or hidden meaning. Assertive communication is a great relationship-builder.

- With aggressive communication, you express your own needs, desires, ideas, and feelings without considering and respecting the needs of others. You promote your own interest at the expense of others and use forceful communication to crush others' viewpoints.

- When you do not express your own needs, desires, ideas, and feelings in situations where it might be advisable to, you use a passive communication style.

- Passive-aggressive communication is, as the name says, a combination of the passive and aggressive styles. It involves being passive in expressing your own needs, desires, ideas, and feelings, but being aggressive in your underlying intent. Passive-aggressive communication often involves not speaking your message, but trying to convey it through small, disrespectful, annoying, or ambiguous comments and actions.

Which communication style do you think has your preference? In the table on the next page, I have categorized some of the typical characteristics of each style to make it easier for you to assess which style you most identify with.

Assertive	Aggressive	Passive	Passive-aggressive
Speak in a calm, clear, and steady voice	Speak in a loud and demanding voice	Speak in an apologetic or submissive manner	Use sarcasm
Make eye contact, smile, and nod	Make piercing eye contact	Avoid eye contact	Use non-verbal behavior (sighing, eye-rolling)
Maintain an open and relaxed posture	Maintain an overbearing posture	Maintain a slumped posture	Use inconsistent facial and body language
Ask for what you want/ need	Demand what you want/need	Give in to others	Act deceptively
Listen so as to hear other people's feelings and needs	Interrupt the other person frequently	Be unable to say no	Listen so as to find ways to subvert the other person

When you use the communication style best suited for the situation, you make the biggest impact. Most situations call for a blend of communication styles. Analyze different situations to see which method of communication will work best through listening and observing. The most important thing is to adjust to the needs of the situation you are in.

Lastly, I want to share with you an insight from the famous TED talk by Amy Cuddy, an American social physiologist who conducted research on body language. Non-verbal communication, or body language, has taken a prominent place in this chapter. It is part of speaking, listening, and interpreting. I shared my mishap with body language in the example of the exam day at the Dutch tax office, and I am sure, if you think deep and hard (or maybe not so deep and hard at all) you can name a few you've made yourself.

According to Cuddy, body language is a form of interaction in which bodies communicate with each other. Research shows that we pass judgement on each other purely based on body language—for instance, when we decide whom to hire or promote, or which political candidate to vote for. Crossing our arms and standing tall is commonly perceived as being powerful and strong. On the other hand, hiding our face behind our hands and looking down is commonly perceived as being powerless and weak.

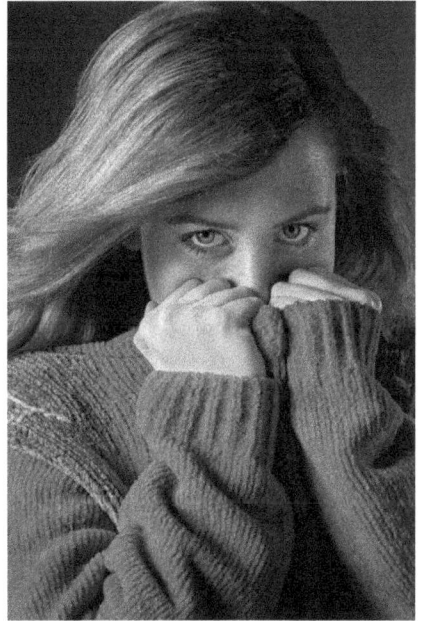

However, according to Cuddy, it is not just others who pass judgment on us in response to our body language—we pass that judgment on ourselves. Our thoughts, feelings, and even physiology change based on our own non-verbal communication. This opens up a whole new practice of influencing your own behavior.

Let's say you tend to be a bit shy when meeting new people. According to Cuddy, if you use power-posing for a couple of minutes just before you walk into a room full of strangers you can tweak your feelings of shyness to become more comfortable walking into the room. Small tweaks like this can become big changes over time.

Key takeaways

- To communicate means to send, receive, and interpret messages in which both sender and receiver take on an active role.

- There are many obstacles to effective communication, which can be grouped into three categories: linguistic, cultural and political.

- Both sender and receiver will have a preferred communication style. You need to know what your own preferred style is and acquire the ability to adjust styles when and where needed.

- Through non-verbal communication, people pass judgement on others as well as on themselves.

SOCIALIZE

lead

know

motivate

communicate

understand

socialize

adapt

Humans engage almost constantly in social behavior. We interact with friends, colleagues, and strangers daily and in highly complex, changing social environments. Whereas communication is about what is being said and received and how this information is interpreted, **socializing** is all about forming basic relationships with others.

Socializing is healthy. We are designed to do it. The body and mind crave connections with other bodies and minds. Behaving socially is the easiest way to curb this craving. It allows you to meet and interact with people and form strong relationships, either privately/personally or in a business context. Some of them could become your biggest supporters and allies. In tough times, the support you can get from them could be vital.

Social behavior depends on a number of different factors. The first one is you. Your personality is a big influencer on how you act toward others. If you are characterized as an introvert, striking up a conversation with someone new might be a daunting activity for

"The meeting of two personalities is like the contact of two chemical substances: if there is any reaction, both are transformed."
—Carl Jung

you. Alternately, if you are characterized as having a strong sense of duty, forming a strong bond with someone who is consistently ten minutes late for meetings might not be a good match. Secondly, your social behavior is dependent on the situation you are in. An annual party at the office is a completely different environment than that of a progress meeting with a client. And thirdly, the behavior of your interaction partner(s) has an influence on your own social behavior. If someone is watching, you might not pick your nose, whereas otherwise you might. All three factors predict your social behavior.

Imagine—it's a Friday evening, and the company's annual business party is ongoing. The canteen is decorated, the lights are dimmed, and the music is loud. You decided, spur of the moment, to stay and attend. Everyone is having a good time. You've had maybe a few too many drinks, but are still steady on your feet and having a marvelous time. It's great to socialize with the team and get to know them better. You feel like they are really warming up to you, and it takes you little effort to get to know more about their lives outside of work. In previous attempts, you had been less successful making this great step forward. The week after, you see differences in the way the team interacts with you. That Wednesday, when you need some of the engineers to finish something late before going home, you notice it takes less effort to convince them to stay.

From the example, it is clear that your own personality had an influence on your social behavior. You decided to stay and have a few drinks ,which made it easier to interact with your team. The behavior of your team also influenced your behavior. The fact that they warmed up to you made you feel confident and have a great time. And the environment also had its effect. The dimly lit room, the music, and the availability of drinks all had an effect on your social behavior. Again, three factors—you, the other, and the environment—all have an influence on your social behavior.

In Chapter 1, we looked at the importance of knowing your-self. If you worked through some of the practices in the chapter, you have become more aware of what you are like. You know if you prefer talking over listening; if you behave in an open or reserved manner; if you approach people easily or first want to see which way the wind blows. All of these are insights into you that influence your social behavior. It is important to understand that these insights influence your behavior, but do not predict it. There is no law stating you have to be a social person to behave sociably. Even if you don't feel like it, you can make the deliberate choice to behave more like a social creature.

Your social behavior is also influenced by the environment you are in and the person(s) you are interacting with. To handle this complexity, you often unconsciously adjust your behavior to fit specific interaction partners, situations, and standards. For example, while a person might dominate a colleague at work, they might also be sensitive to the needs of their child. Although this sounds pretty simple, just imagine a small child navigating the world. They are blissfully unaware of the pressures of unspoken standards and rules. This is not so different for many adults. Culture and upbringing define how we perceive the environments we navigate and the ways in which we interact with others. For this, we use three main processes: social seeing, social thinking, and social doing.

Seeing   *Thinking*   *Doing*

- **Social seeing** involves picking up on social clues. It means noticing the context: Is a setting casual or formal? Are the others close friends, acquaintances, or strangers? Different situations call for different kinds of behavior and also for seeing different kinds of behavior in others. If something happens that is inappropriate for its context, such as drinking too much, monitoring others' reactions will allow you to change course.

- **Social thinking** involves interpretation of others' behavior to understand why someone is doing what they are doing or why something is happening. Is something meant as playful or aggressive? Is something deliberate or accidental? Why is a certain reaction instigating a change in the situation? It also involves predicting likely responses and coming up with an effective strategy to influence desired outcomes.

- **Social doing** means interacting with others in positive ways. Some people might know what to do, but still have trouble actually doing it. For instance, they might want to join in on a conversation at a network event, but feel anxious and freeze when they actually need to make the move. Acting on impulses in these kinds of situations is not uncommon.

Examples of social behavior include:

- ✓ Shaking hands
- ✓ Flirting
- ✓ Making conversation
- ✓ Sharing a meal
- ✓ Coaching
- ✓ Cooperating
- ✓ Offering reassurance
- ✓ And more

They all contribute to your ability to set up successful relationships and long-lasting bonds, which are essential to your life satisfaction and feeling of accomplishment. This is the case for all humans alike.

In the project world, no one accomplishes anything alone. It is a fantasy to believe that you, as the project manager, are going to make all the difference on your own. It takes the effort of the entire project team to make a project a success. A project is therefore more so a social system than anything else.

This makes the bonds between people even more important than you might have thought. Just imagine: Who would you go the extra mile for? The project manager who only speaks to you when they want to hear about results and progress? Or the one who asks you about your weekend activities at the coffee machine in the morning? I think the answer for most of us is very clear. Having a great bond with the project team helps you when the project is strained and overtime is required. Creating some leeway with the

"If I have the opportunity to really have a laugh with someone it makes it so much easier to work together."
—Mirjam van der Plas, Associate Director Advisory Group Health, Safety & Environment, the Netherlands

client through a good relationship helps you get that extra budget for some of the variations you have encountered. Successful relationships lead to strong alliances, which in turn lead to enhanced influence on the project outcome. It is as simple as that.

In the introduction of the book, I told you about when I started taking more notice and care of the people in my projects. It was during a difficult time that I let go of the rigor of only managing the project budget and schedule and started understanding the power of strong relationships. I made a deliberate choice to behave more sociably in an effort to form bonds with the people around me. It enhanced my socializing skills, allowing me to easily navigate the social environments of the cultures and industries I've worked in since. However, even nowadays, I still find certain social situations difficult. I was at a conference on Artificial Intelligence a few months back and did not speak to anyone. I felt so uncomfortable with the topic that I did not dare to strike up a conversation. Other conferences can be super fun and engaging. This is the world we live in.

Sociability is the quality of liking to meet and spend time in other people's company. If extraversion is part of your personality, sociability might come easy to you. If you tend to be more introverted, perhaps it won't. As I mentioned before, this does not have to be an issue. You can make the deliberate choice to act sociable and strike up or enter a conversation, even if this makes you naturally uncomfortable. Just keep in mind that having successful relationships with the people around you will make you happier and will help you get one step closer to achieving the project goal. Some strategies that will help you increase your sociability are the following:

▪ *Try to look trustworthy*

The very first thing someone will try to determine about you is whether you can be trusted. Expressing warmth by smiling and looking someone in the eyes is the easiest way to guide their decision to trust you. It might sound very simplistic, but just imagine someone coming up to you without smiling. Would you feel inclined to start a conversation with this person? I don't think so. Expressing warmth makes you appear so much more welcoming and open to engage with.

▪ *Ask open-ended questions*

Once you've entered a conversation, it is time to talk. If you don't want the spotlight during a conversation to be on you (all the time), get familiar with asking open-ended questions. It will encourage others to talk. Open-ended questions start with "who," "what," "where," "when," "how," or "why." Again, be cautious with "why" questions, as they could result in defensiveness. Examples related to projects could be:

- ✓ How did you end up in project management?

- ✓ What projects did you work on before this one?

- ✓ What do you like about this project?

- ✓ How can I help you get this done?

- ✓ Who do you think should lead the meeting?

■ ***Encourage others to talk about themselves***

Most people enjoy talking about themselves. Asking a question about someone's family, hobbies, or career is a great way of keeping a conversation going. Showing you are interested by actively listening is a great way to keep a conversation going.

■ ***Don't control yourself all of the time***

Remember the example of the company's annual business party from the beginning of the chapter? Needing alcohol or something stronger to become more sociable is not uncommon. It is a way of eliminating the barriers in someone's head that make them control their behavior. Try to turn this off. Simply enjoy being with people without questioning everything you are going to say or do over and over in your head.

"Sociability is the glue between people."
—Pierre Henquet, Project Manager, Belgium

The ability to grasp the complexity of the person(s) you are interacting with and the environment you are in is the next part of your ability to socialize. This part is governed not only by your own behavior, but also by that of the other person(s), which in turn is again affected by the context of the environment. Having a strategy in your back pocket for anything that can happen is unattainable. It is all about having enough understanding of the beliefs and standards of the environment you are in and trusting you are up for the task. Embracing awkward moments and rejection is part of this. You won't like everybody you meet, nor will others. You won't feel comfortable in every environment, nor will others. There are a couple of things to keep in mind, though, when entering a situation, that will help you not set yourself up for immediate failure:

- Do some upfront investigation. Whether you are going to a new business site abroad or meeting a new supplier at your office, try to find out some more about the company and people you are about to meet. You can find heaps of information on the internet these days. You can also ask around if other people have had any experiences. Knowing a bit more about the company and someone's background and interests means you are doing your job to try to avoid awkward interactions.

- Try to be fair. Doing upfront investigation does not mean you need to have an opinion. If you've passed judgement before a word has been exchanged, you will unconsciously look for confirming evidence. This is called confirmation bias. Try to remain openminded at all times.

- Take your time. Don't rush to conclusions when it comes to social situations. Think about the circumstances that might influence behavior. The rudeness of a first encounter can be a result of nerves or fear of rejection. Perhaps a person might be very likeable once you get to know them a bit better.

Setting goals will act as a driving force in your development and hold you accountable. There is no need to start big. It can be anything from 'start a conversation with someone you don't know' to 'go to an event and follow up on a connection you made.' Try out things in relation to your own behavior as well as different interaction partners and environments. Little by little, you will get better and have more fun with it. Here's an example of how I made small goals work for me in my time in Norway:

I shared with you at the very beginning of the book that I was lonely the first year I spend in Norway. I decided to put more focus into socializing with people and building positive relationships to overcome my loneliness. I knew that the easiest way to do this was at work, as I was spending five days a week their anyway. But I also enlisted the help of initiatives like Couchsurfing and Meetup to meet people on the weekends.

For work, I set myself the small goal to attend lunch at the canteen a minimum of once a week. My very first lunch was very uncomfortable. I walked into the room feeling very self-conscious. While everyone looked at me, I rushed to a table to sit down and eat. Awkward! But going into the

lunchroom the following week was already easier. And as time passed, I spent more time eating my lunch with my colleagues then at my desk in my office. I actually enjoyed being away from the pressure of the projects for half an hour a day and having a laugh with people. It took another ten months before I got invited on the first "jente tur," which literally translates into "ladies trip." I went to a logwood cabin in the Norwegian mountains for a weekend with colleagues to hike and enjoy each other's company. This is an example of how small goals and steps over time can make a big impact.

Aside from overall life satisfaction, one of the main reasons for social behavior as a project manager is to build strong alliances. These alliances can result in mutual benefit either within your company, among clients and suppliers, or more broadly within your industry and field. In management terms, we call this your network. Many diverse opportunities can arise through this:

- Your network can be a great source of new information. Knowledge sharing among people is very common, and not only in a work context. By actively investing in your networking, you get access to different perspectives and ideas.

- Your network can be a great source of job security. A study by Granovetter (1995) shows over 50 percent of jobs are filled though personal contacts. Maintaining good relationships with people from other companies can land you your next job or contract.

- Networking can help you identify the right individuals or companies to fit your project. Knowing they are qualified and capable of delivering based on personal experience is a valuable asset to utilize. These could be suppliers for equipment and parts, or sources of external expertise in the form of contractors.

Building a network takes time. The longer you are in the job, the more people you meet, and the bigger your network gets. However, time is not the only factor influencing the value of your network. If you don't treat the people you meet well, it does not matter how many people you know. Follow up on how individuals in your network are doing by giving them a call or sending them an email. Actively share your knowledge and experiences, and offer assistance when you can. Following up and following through are the keys to building a strong network.

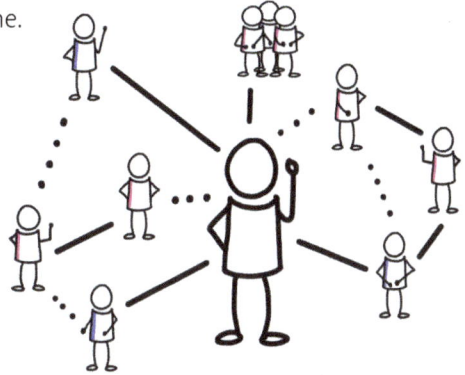

An example on the power of a network from my own life:

I've been in the process of building my very first house in the Dutch countryside. I started building at the end of 2017 and I am currently (mid-2019) almost done. I am super happy with the way it's turned out, and I can't wait to move in. However, without utilities like electricity and water, I will not be able to move.

In the Netherlands, all work related to the utilities grid is centrally regulated by the government. There is a website where people can apply, after which the work is distributed over the various provinces to be executed by a local contractor. At the beginning of March, I completed the application. The earliest possible appointment for the initial check of the house was three months out. This was a setback, but not something I thought I could do something about.

That is, until last week, six weeks after I completed the application. The owner of a construction company I hired to do some work suggested a workaround. He knew a guy at the local contractor and was willing to give him a call to see if he could pull some strings to get me scheduled in earlier. Two days later, the local contractor showed up at my house to do the initial check. Everything was okay, and I am now penciled in for utilities connection within the next three weeks. This is just one example of the power of a strong network!

One of the project professionals I interviewed gave me another example of the power of a network:

"I have been working in the event Industry for many years. It is a business in which people tend to know each other, and where last-minute changes are not uncommon. I was working with a small team on a big event some years back. Everything was in order and arranged for the event

to take place, when all of a sudden, three days before the event, one of the main acts dropped out. We had to adapt immediately. Making changes to social media, etc. was an easy fix. However, the printed materials for the day itself had already been made. The printing company said they could not make a three-day turnaround for new materials work. So I went into my network. I'd worked with other printing companies before, and it didn't take long for me to find the right person to help us out. As I had worked with them on a number of other prior projects, I knew their worth and how to communicate with them. This made defusing a tough situation much easier. On the morning of the event, the new materials arrived. We worked with the team to make sure everything was in its right place before the doors opened—a successful diversion of a disaster due to a great network of support."

"It is a pre-requisite to have social skills to make connections with people. However, you ultimately want to find out what really drives each individual, both on a personal and professional level."
—Bengt-Olof Klemp,
Managing Director, Germany

Key takeaways

- Socializing is about forming relationships with the people we interact with. This can be friends, colleagues, or strangers.

- Your social behavior is dependent on your own personality, the environment you are in, and the behavior of the person(s) you are interacting with.

- There is no law stating you have to be sociable to act social.

- Relationships lead to strong alliances, which are vital when times get tough.

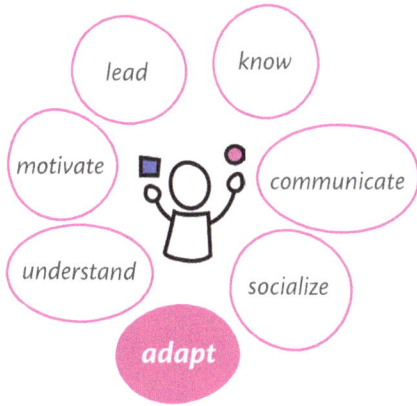

ADAPT

I n the capricious project arena, I have on many occasions referred to myself as a chameleon. I changed the way I spoke, acted, or dressed based on the demands of the environment or situation I was in. For a while, I got lost in this turmoil, unsure what of 'me' remained. Through self-development and working with a coach, I realized that the changes I made were deliberate choices to talk or act in ways best suited for the challenges at hand, instead of becoming less of me. Like a chameleon who adjusts to the colors of its environment, I was equipping myself with a variety of colors as well, to be able to adapt my behavior to best suit the demands of the environment or challenge at hand without questioning or changing myself. The next skill of the People Factor is **adapt.**

"We cannot solve our problems with the same thinking we used when we created them."
—Albert Einstein

Before I elaborate on the skill to adapt, I want to touch upon the ability to manage your behavior first. My ability to utilize a variety of behaviors, i.e. access many different colors like the chameleon, only arose after I learned to have more control over my impulsive behavior. Using reflection and feedback practices, I became aware of my character and beliefs and how my experiences have shaped some of the triggers I have. This was a long process of trial and error, in which even today on occasion I submit to a proverbial dagger throw. Knowing myself and having the ability to (on many occasions) control my emotions and impulses has helped me achieve some of the bigger goals I set myself in life. As will you!

Self-control is a complex cognitive process that requires the presence of self-knowledge before it can be developed. More specifically, we need to learn to identify our emotions, understand how they affect us, and then control them. Self-control is not about hiding emotions or not paying attention to them, hoping they will magically disappear. Developing self-control is about making a conscious decision to not let yourself be driven by emotions and impulses, instead teaching yourself to manage them properly.

Primary emotions like joy, anger, sadness, or fear are often easily identified, as they manifest quite obviously in our body. It is common for someone who feels happy to look for positive experiences while someone who is sad only wants to disconnect. Secondary emotions are not that obvious, though, and are a result of one or more primary emotions. To use myself as an example, I feel a primary emotion of anger when someone treats other people in an unequal way. If, for instance, an intern assigned to the project is in a subtle way bullied into getting coffee during a meeting, the hairs on the back of my neck stand up. The secondary emotion I experience related to this is still a version of fear, however—a fear of missing out. This fear was cultivated during my very traditional upbringing, where men and women were not seen and treated as equals, an experience that has never left me.

See if you can catch yourself in the act when reflecting on experiencing emotions and impulses during situations, and ask others for feedback. You can make use of the exercise below to assess situations as well:

What came before the emotion or impulsive behavior?	What was the specific emotion or impulsive behavior?	What happened after the specific emotion or impulsive behavior?
Where was I? Who was there with me? What was happening?	What did I feel? What behavior did I display?	What did I feel afterward? What did I do or say afterward?

You could add other situations in which the same emotion or impulsive behavior happened. For instance, if you keep feeling anxious in your project, write down the specific situations to find the triggers. Identify what purpose the emotion or impulsive behavior has and why you think it appeared.

Once you are aware of your emotions and impulsive behavior, it is time to try and control it. This is the most difficult part. You want to find activities or ways to reduce the symptoms of the emotions you are feeling. Two strategies to consider are:

- Find ways to create distance by distracting yourself from what causes the emotion. For example, you can do a quick breathing exercise, count to ten, or leave the meeting to go to the restroom for a few minutes until you feel ready to face it. Distance might result in a new perspective on the cause of the emotion.

■ Test yourself by experimenting in situations where triggers are present. Seek out the grey areas, and pay attention to the different results you get by acting differently.

I received the following example of a project manager I interviewed practicing self-control:

"I am aware of how I react in certain situations when it comes to an engineer in my company. I have been working with him on different projects for a year now, and there are two or three things in his behavior that just boil me. They keep reoccurring, week after week, and I know them. Certain days, I am really able to pace it out and discuss it and do it well. But certain days, I don't. I know I have this reflex, so I am aware of my impulses, but I can't always control them.'

Self-control is one of the most difficult skills for anyone to manage. Just look at the obesity rates in the Western world. Or the amount of drug users worldwide. Self-control is also about allowing yourself to not always do it well. This doesn't say anything more about you than that you are human. Your willingness to try to do better next time is all you need to progress.

One of the project professionals I spoke to gave me the following insight when talking about self-control:

"I was working on a project as a client project manager. The relationship between the client and a major supplier was weak from the start and had become more strained as the project was moving into its final stages. I anticipated a schedule overrun of four months based on a breakdown of the remaining work, and I brought this up with the supplier on several occasions. The supplier, however, assured me there was no risk, they had full control. So I let it go.

One Friday evening, an email came in from the supplier with a variation order for four months of delay and its associated cost. The email asked if we could please approve the variation immediately so they could start working against the new schedule to ensure they would have a chance to reach the new completion date. A bomb exploded within my company. That evening, I initiated talks with the project sponsor and senior management to come up with a strategy for how to respond. We agreed to bring it up in the next meeting to see what could be done to get rid of the variation. The project sponsor would attend the meeting as well for support.

The meeting started off bad. The supplier had taken one of its senior managers to participate as well, and both he and the project sponsor had difficulties practicing self-control. Without sharing details, the meeting ended with an angry project sponsor storming out. In hindsight, this was a crucial moment in the project. It resulted in an unwillingness to meet halfway in many of the schedule and cost decisions that followed. It locked down the project and resulted in more delay and additional costs.

I spoke with the project sponsor some years after the project finished. Talking about the particular meeting, he offered up his behavior as non-productive in getting the variation order mitigated. Since that time he had reflected on what the trigger had been for him and had been working on controlling it better."

Another of the project professionals I interviewed shared another example:

"I am very serious about my profession. I make deliberate choices to develop my knowledge and skills and put maximum effort toward my performance. I can get really annoyed at people who don't do this. And this annoyance often doesn't go unnoticed. I am very aware of the fact that I get annoyed about others like this, but often the feeling is there too late for me to control. And then I just have to say something, which isn't always smart and has gotten me in trouble.

As an example, I prepared a big change order for a customer a while back, which took me a couple of weeks to prepare. During a meeting some weeks later to negotiate the change, I got the impression they hadn't reviewed it. I asked a couple of sample questions to confirm my suspicion and concluded they had only looked at the executive summary. They challenged me on some variations I had listed in the change order based on not knowing the full extent and intent of the variations. At one point, I just could not contain my frustration anymore and basically called them out on wasting everyone's time. The change order was denied, and the meeting ended. Looking back, I should have controlled my frustrations and focused on getting the change order approved."

Now that we have looked at some strategies and examples to practice self-control, let's go back to the skill this chapter focuses on: adapt. To determine how many colors of the chameleon you need, it is important to grasp the complexity of projects. The Collins English dictionary defines complexity as "the state or quality of being intricate or complex," where complex is defined as "made up of many interconnecting parts." I am sure you can all relate to this if you think of complexity in your projects. Although much research has been done to define the complexity footprint of projects, this hasn't resulted in one overarching theory or model. It seems therefore plausible to state that the development and experience of the project manager result in their own perception of the complexity of projects.

Over the course of my career, I've been in some very complex situations. I spend a lot of time deconstructing situations into smaller, tangible pieces to make them more manageable. Based on this practice, it is my perception that there are three elements that make up complexity in projects:

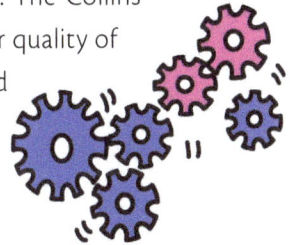

"Nothing is particularly hard if you divide it into smaller jobs."
—Henry Ford

1. **People**. This first element consists of social, cultural, and cognitive complexity. Examples are the number and diversity of people interacting and working with each other, each bringing their own history and experiences into the project, and the level to which self-awareness and the forming of a team and identity are possible.

2. **Process**. This second element consists of the turbulence of the total amount of parts in the project process and the degree of clarity of how the interfaces between these parts are visible, monitored, and controlled. You can see this as the flightpath of an airplane. It can be off-course along the way, but it needs to be right on target when it comes to landing. The project lifecycle is like this: aimed at the target and changeable up until the end.

3. **Content**. This final element consists of the level of scientific and technological knowledge and experience required to complete the project. Examples are the uniqueness of the scope or the environment in which the project is carried out. I worked in an industry in which manufactured equipment is installed three thousand meters below sea level. The extreme requirements of this environment had an effect on the complexity of the project.

All three elements are interconnected and, to various degrees, part of all project challenges you might face. Your ability to recognize what elements make up the complexity of a specific situation allows you to decide what the most appropriate approach could be. One of the project professionals I spoke to gave me an example of the importance of recognizing the elements of complexity:

"As a project sponsor, I was responsible for an overarching manufacturing scope consisting of a main package and some sub-packages. For the big package, I decided to hire an independent project manager. I ended up with two interesting candidates. One had a technical education and background and was certified in a well-known project management method. The other was mostly practical and self-educated. I decided to hire the first candidate.

In the beginning stages of the project, he seemed to be doing well. There were no big issues, and the project planning was on track. However, as time went by, he started complaining more and more about some of the engineers on the team. As these engineers were crucial experts whom we could not afford to lose, I decided to participate in some meetings to find out what was going on.

To my surprise, the project manager kept getting stuck in content discussions with the engineers over small details. He prioritized out-arguing them on the technical solutions required instead of guiding them through the process of coming up with a solution. I spent some weeks providing feedback to the project manager on how his own approach and behavior were affecting the issues he was having. When I myself in the end started getting into similar discussions with him, I decided this could not go on. I went back to the project manager who narrowly missed the cut and hired her to take over control of the engineering team. To my surprise, she resolved some of the dragging issues very quickly by listening to everyone and making decisions to take small steps forward. In the end, I decided to let go of the educated project manager, which was a great decision for the project.

After he was gone the team flourished again, and the proj-
ect had a chance to recover."

Being aware that there are limits to what you can know about
the people, process, and content elements of projects is the first
step to managing them. To handle the uncertainty that remains, you
need to be aware of everything and pay equal attention to all of it,
on top of having the right mindset and skills to continuously adapt.

In a perfect world, you implement the project plan, work with
the project team to formulate the schedule, keep track of progress, and communicate this to the client. Everything goes well, and
everyone just charges along. Of course, no one lives in a
perfect world, and rarely does everything go according to plan. Work takes longer than expected, team
conflicts soar, and technical glitches arise. You
are responsible for getting the project back on
track. Deviation from what was originally planned
is a necessity. You have to articulate the need for
significant change, align everyone involved to the
new direction, and motivate them to work together
to overcome hurdles produced by the change, all with the purpose
of realizing the new goal. You have to do this independent of how
many times this has changed already.

You need to equip yourself for change to happen at any
time—and all the time. This makes a lot of people downright
uncomfortable, including people in your project team. It is your
responsibility to be at the forefront of change and inspire others
through your own mindset and behavior. You need to be able to
think and make decisions quickly and know how to rally the project team to make results happen. One day, this could mean giving
someone free reign to be creative in finding a solution for a deadline

that needs to be met. The next day, the deadline could be moved out, meaning new tasks need to be assigned and structure provided. Adaptability provides a smart approach to these kinds of problems by recognizing complexity and ambiguity in situations through interactions and responsiveness.

Once a complex and ambiguous situation occurs, the first thing you need to do is let yourself recover from the shock and turbulence that arises from the situation. Your ability to absorb change by keeping the range of options open and dealing with the unexpected future are crucial to adopting the change. You need the ability to bounce back; you need **resilience**.

Resilience is the ability to cope with and handle the challenges and setbacks you meet in the course of your life, whether in your private life or in a project. The ability to bounce back stronger from the stress of surprises, setbacks, disappointments, and failure is critical to your skill to adapt.

> "The greatest glory in living lies not in never falling, but in rising every time we fall."
> —Nelson Mandela

Resilience can be taught. It involves developing thoughts and behaviors that allow you to recover from stressful events. How resilient you are is relative and depends on the situation you're in. You may, for example, be very resilient in your workplace, while being not resilient at all when it comes to personal relationships. This can change over time depending on your interactions and the environment you are in. As you become more resilient, so too do you develop your ability to adapt.

There are several ways to improve your resilience. Having a good support system, maintaining positive relationships, and having a positive self-image and optimistic attitude are some of them. A way to better understand the concept of resilience, and a great way to build it, is the four-factor approach created by Senari. The approach consists of the following four factors:

1. State the facts;

2. Place blame where it belongs, if it is needed at all;

3. Reframe;

4. Take your time.

Let's assume you face the following challenge:

> At the start of your project, you made sure to translate the business goal of remaining within budget into smaller, tangible goals for the project team to work toward. Because of this, you have been able to make a large amount of savings by developing opportunities and following them through with the team. Due to some of the choices you made, however, the project is running into some tangible schedule delays. The extra cost for longer execution can be covered by the savings, so you are comfortable with this. During the monthly review with senior management, you get told the schedule delay needs to be mitigated; you need to end up at the original target date. The sales as a result from the finished project have been forecasted for the new year, and not being able to produce has been qualified as a major business risk. It's the first time you hear about this, and to say you are upset would be an understatement. You have no clue how you are going to make reaching both goals happen.

Using the four-factor approach by Senari, you would start by simply listening to or talking about what happened without magnifying it. For example, you might say to yourself: "I have been given an additional goal by management and will need to find a way to meet this goal."

The second step involves taking ownership and not placing blame. Instead of blaming management or yourself, you could simply say: "Ok, I've got a new goal. This happened, things happen. Although it is perhaps a bit late in the project, I have no visibility or control over the implications for the business or the implications for the project. I will do everything within my power to make it work."

The third step involves reframing and re-evaluating the event in your mind. You could also call this looking for the silver lining. It could always have been worse—for instance, you could have gotten two new goals. Or senior management could have decided to give the project to someone else instead. They obviously have confidence in you being able to reach the target date, otherwise they would not have asked you. Reframing involves looking for the bright side of a situation and being grateful for something.

The final step involves giving yourself some time to recover and adapt. You need this time to come up with a new strategy and to get charged to rally the team toward the additional goal.

Engaging in this simple process will train your brain to think and look at situations differently. It will help you cope with the challenges and setbacks you meet over the course of the project. Training the brain to be resilient is not enough on its own, however. Your body has an important part to play in developing resilience as well. You don't want to set yourself up for fatigue or potential burnout. Exercise provides a great opportunity for stress relief, as does going out more. Seeking solitude and retreating into nature are also great ways to escape from the turmoil and stimuli of busy project life. The more you engage in the process, the more resilient you will become.

The second thing you want to do when a complex and ambiguous situation occurs is show **flexibility**. Flexibility relates to the variety you are able to bring to the table. It implies a diversity of potential solutions and options, which all require a diversity of approaches, attitudes, and behaviors.

Flexibility is one of your best friends in projects, as it helps you to stabilize a situation when crisis could strike. To develop your flexibility, keep the following in mind:

- Your skills-box needs to be full

Your ability to use both traditional best practices and skills from the People Factor means you have at your disposal a wide variety of solutions, options, attitudes, and behaviors. Use the skills at your disposal, and stay curious at all times to new things you could learn. Apply situational learning when you experience complexity related to people, process, and content in your projects to keep enhancing your skills.

- Train yourself in breaking down a situation into manageable pieces

Your ability to deconstruct a complex situation into the three main components—people, process, and content—allows you to pick the correct skill(s) for the situation at hand. By systematically investigating the various components, you stay best equipped to take the most appropriate way forward. Also, don't forget to support others in reducing complexity.

"As a project manager you need the ability to simplify difficult situations so that neither you nor others get lost in the project jungle."
—Bengt-Olof Klemp, Managing
Director, Germany

- Stay open-minded at all times

Your willingness to consider new ideas and different perspectives helps you manage the uncertainty of a challenging situation. It deflates, not just for you but also for others. Stop thinking in black-and-white terms. And don't let your brain trick you into taking shortcuts based on your experiences. You want to have access to a variety of solutions, options ,and approaches when deciding on the best way forward.

- Utilize your values

Your values keep you grounded in challenging situations that are often accompanied by discomfort and stress. Taking on the responsibility for designing a way forward is something different than making an ethically dubious decision. Listen, and trust your gut feeling to tell you what is right.

- Learn from others

An excellent way to develop flexibility is by learning from others. Surround yourself with colleagues or peers who show excellent flexibility, so you can learn from them. The more you isolate yourself, the more you will brood over bad decisions.

One of the project professionals I spoke to shared with me the following example of flexibility:

"I was working as a project manager on a project for a client executing the expansion of the production capacity of an innovate new product. The company had been around for almost ten years by that time and had retained some of its innovative culture from its early years. The flexibility of this culture could be found throughout the company and therefore in the project as well.

The full scope of the project was broken down into various smaller contracts and outsourced to various contractors. The construction portion was outsourced to a very traditional construction company, which resulted in a culture clash between the two companies.

We kept thinking outside of the box when it came to reaching our goals. The schedule was tough, and the fixed budget made it necessary, in our opinion, to remain openminded and creative in finding new ways to remain on track. The contractor, however, functioned according to standard processes and approaches, and was not able to be flexible in methods of working. Although the people on-site kept trying to meet us halfway, the company itself was just not resilient and flexible enough to adapt."

"When you are able to adjust for instance your language and way of working you will be able to keep the team united."
—Yannick Avril, Director of Engineering
& Construction for Asia Pacific, China

Key takeaways

- Your ability to adapt depends on your ability to control your emotions and impulsive behavior.

- Self-control is a practice of trial and error that solely depends on your willingness to improve.

- Complexity in projects consists of three elements: people, process, and content.

- Being able to adapt means developing both resilience and flexibility.

UNDERSTAND

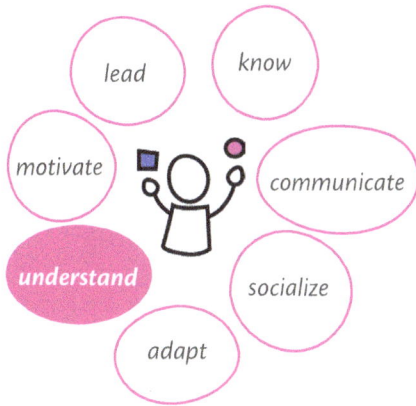

T he next skill of the People Factor is **understand.** Understand means you know enough about something to adequately deal with it. In the context of projects, this means that you, as a project manager, need to understand the meaning and importance of values and the impact of culture on behavior.

"Better to understand a little than to misunderstand a lot."
—Lord Chesterfield

Values

In Chapter 1, I explained that according to McAdams (1996), one of the prominent parts of knowing yourself and others is character- istic adaptations. Examples of characteristic adaptations are someone's desires, beliefs, concerns, and values. According to research, having clarity of values is an important catalyst for success in both personal and business life. Values take up a prominent role in management research and curriculum and are, according to Elvis Presley, "fingerprints that you leave on everything you do." As a project manager, it is therefore crucial for you to understand the meaning and importance of values.

Values are part of the deepest level of our personal programming. They are fundamental beliefs that motivate our attitudes and actions, meaning they serve as general guidelines for our behavior. Values inform our thoughts and words and drive purposeful action, which helps us grow and develop. Generally, we are largely predisposed to adopt the values we were raised with, which reflect the culture we were raised in. We tend to believe these values to be 'right,' although they might lead to clashes in preferences and priorities.

Some values have intrinsic worth, such as freedom, truth, and love. The actions resulting from these intrinsic values make you feel good. Other values, such as ambition, responsibility, and courage describe behavior that is instrumental as a means to an end. Actions resulting from such values make you look good. There are also so-called sacred values. These aren't factors to be weighed during decision-making, but rather duties that cannot be compromised on. For some people, for example, their nation's flag may represent a sacred value, while for others, this flag may just be a piece of cloth. Values in any sense vary among individuals and across cultures, and tend to shift through the course of our lives.

To give you a better understanding of what values are, have a look at the compiled list on the next page. The list is not exhaustive—it's just something to get you started on understanding the scope of values.

Living by our personal values might sound easy in theory. After all, values are, simply put, the things that are important to us in our lives, the things that guide our actions, so it should be natural to live by them. However, most of us don't truly know our values. We don't understand what's most important to us. Instead, we focus on what our society, culture, and media value. Uncovering your values

Accountability	Fairness	Leadership	Security
Adventure	Freedom	Learning	Self-respect
Ambition	Fulfillment	Legacy	Service
Authenticity	Generosity	Optimism	Simplicity
Belonging	Growth	Order	Spirituality
Collaboration	Harmony	Patience	Success
Commitment	Health	Peace	Teamwork
Competence	Honesty	Perseverance	Tradition
Connection	Humility	Perfection	Trust
Contribution	Inclusion	Power	Truth
Cooperation	Independence	Pride	Understanding
Dignity	Integrity	Recognition	Uniqueness
Diversity	Intelligence	Reliability	Usefulness
Environment	Joy	Respect	Vision
Equality	Justice	Responsibility	Vulnerability
Ethics	Kindness	Risk-taking	Wealth
Family	Knowledge	Safety	Wisdom

and consistently living by and through them is a practice of conscious decision-making. For example, let's say you value adventure. Career choices that include travel or starting your own business may be appropriate choices for you. However, you feel like 'safe' choices are more appropriate, as you have your spouse and kids to think of. You end up feeling smothered by the 'safe' job you are in. Or, on the other hand, if you value security, you might feel insecure and crave a more settled life instead of jumping at the opportunity to travel the world. Being curious about and ultimately naming what our values are can make for a much easier life in that way.

According to research by Brené Brown (2018), each person has only a few deep-rooted intrinsic values. These values do not shift dependent on context; rather, they take on different meaning in different settings or situations. So, independent from whether you are at home, in school, or in the office, your values do not change. Just as you have your personal values, so too do the people around you. One of the challenges of living by our values is those moments when our own values clash with those of the people around us. Let's look at an example:

> In a project with an impossible deadline, a mechanical engineer was tasked with the responsibility to design and procure the entire mechanical scope for a plant. As the mechanical engineer was getting overwhelmed by all the work at hand, the electrical engineer offered to help out and take over the workload for the design and the ordering of the pumps. Over the course of the next month, the electrical engineer worked together with suppliers to get the design of the pumps fixed so that ordering could happen. By that time, tension between the two men had risen, mainly due to the rapidly approaching decision time for ordering. One Friday, the deadline was finally there, and the mechanical

engineer was unavailable to approve the final ordering. After deliberating with the project manager on what to do, the electrical engineer made the decision to order the pumps. Returning to the office on Monday morning, he received a public scolding from the mechanical engineer for having made such a decision without his approval.

You might think that the project manager should have taken the decision to handle the ordering into their own hands instead of leaving it with the electrical engineer. Or that the project manager should have agreed to move out the deadline to the next week, when both men were in. Although I agree there would be value to these approaches, that is not the particular reason for using this example—this is about understanding the meaning and importance of values. The underlying issue between the two men had nothing to do with the project goals, but rather with behavior resulting from a misalignment in values. The public scolding part of the example is where the problem lies. The electrical engineer was so hurt and offended on a values level due to the public scolding by the mechanical engineer that cooperation between the two men after that point turned out to be difficult. Every action by the project manager was taken to try to get the two men back on speaking terms but unfortunately without result. The issue had its effect not only on the two engineers involved but also on the rest of the team present. Trust in the team was diminished, and it was never fully restored again.

Clarity of values is as important among the project team as it is for the project manager themself. Specifically, the bigger the overlap of personal values and project values, the better the performance, which in turn directly influences the project outcome. This overlap is called shared project values. It is the task of the project manager to establish shared values that everyone can agree upon and conform to. Examples of shared project values are trust, integrity, and continuous learning.

The two areas of values important in the context of this chapter are your personal values and the establishing of shared project values. You perhaps have already reflected on your personal values as part of the 'know' chapter. If not (or if not enough), let's have a look at how to uncover your personal values first.

Without going through a discovery process, it is challenging to identify your personal values. It is easy to speculate and idealize about what values work best for you or what you should value. But knowing and accepting what you value takes effort. You need self-honesty, patience, and determination to get there. Before you start the process, make sure you start with a beginner's mind. Take a deep breath, and empty your mind. Remember that your conscious mind does not have all the answers. You want to allow yourself space for your inner truth to give you insights and revelations.

A good place to start when uncovering your personal values is the question, "What makes me feel good?" For example, if telling the truth makes you feel good, perhaps honesty is one of your personal values. Or, if you see someone being demeaning to the cleaning staff, and that makes you feel bad, equality might be a personal value you hold in high regard. Here are some other questions you might want to ask yourself as well:

- ✓ What is important to me in life?

- ✓ If I could do anything, without having to worry about practicalities such as money, what would give me fulfillment?

- ✓ What stories or behaviors inspire me?

- ✓ What stories or behaviors make me angry?

✓ What do I want to change about the world, or about myself?

✓ What am I most proud of?

✓ When was I the happiest in life?

If one of your answers includes "being good at my job," then competence or growth might be important values for you. Or, if you wrote, "doing the right thing," then you might value justice.

You might end up with a list of twenty or thirty values, which is too many to be accountable to. It is time to organize them into related groups. For example, values like responsibility, accountability, and punctuality relate to each other. And values like family, connection, and inclusiveness are related as well. Group them together.

Next, highlight the central theme of each group you have compiled. This can be one of the values from the group—it doesn't need to be a new value or word to encompass them all. Keep the other values, as they provide context to your primary value. Now comes the most difficult part. It is time to shave down your list, so you are left with only two or three primary values, and perhaps a few supporting ones. There is no magic number when it comes to how many values you should end up with. But keep in mind, you are trying to uncover what values really matter to you in life so you can live by them. Living by too many values will only result in not taking real advantage of them. Here are a few potential questions to help you shave down your list:

✓ Which value(s) on your list are essential to your life?

✓ Which value(s) on your list support your inner self?

✓ Which value(s) on your list represent your primary way of being?

Rank the values you are left with in order of importance. This is another difficult task, but remember, you do not need to compile your list in one day. Put your list aside and sleep on it. See how you feel the next day, or leave the list for a few more days. It's your process—see what feels right to you.

Once you have your shortlist composed, it's time to translate your values into specific behaviors. This step is perhaps even more important than being crystal clear on what your values actually are. If you don't walk the walk, your values don't mean anything, right? To test if your behavior is aligned with the values you picked, you can use the following questions for each value:

- ✓ What are three behaviors that support my value?

- ✓ What are three slippery behaviors that are outside of my value?

- ✓ What examples can I name of times when I was fully utilizing my value?

If your behavior does not match your shortlist of values, you want to set yourself goals to align them. These goals can become an integrated part of your self-reflection practices, as related in Chapter 1. Write down your strategy and progress in your journal, and revisit your shortlist on a periodic basis. It will give you focus and get you that much closer to purposeful behavior and actions in your personal and business lives.

A project professional I interviewed gave me this following example about personal values:

"I was lucky to start my career in a small, family-owned company with 120 employees. I was responsible for running turnkey contracts and had to report to the owner every month as part of the project reviews. In this company, I really learned that the money I was spending wasn't my money, and that I had to manage this correctly, which was in line with my own personal and family value of not wasting money. If I were to lose a lot of money on my projects, I knew it would have an immediate and direct effect on myself and my colleagues.

Afterward, transitioning into a big company, it was quite surprising how different this sometimes was. I feel very grateful for having had this experience, as I feel I would not have felt so responsible for not losing too much money without it. Some of my success thus far is due to being able to remain committed to this value."

Now that you understand how to uncover your own values, and perhaps have already done so, it is easier to guide the establishment of shared values across your project. Keep in mind the example of the two engineers and the mechanical pump scope. It is your task to make sure everyone in your team can agree upon shared project values. These values do not have to be aligned with everyone's personal values. They are a set of guidelines for behavior and cooperation that everyone agrees upon. Examples include openness, transparency, quality, holding one another accountable, and respect.

"The ambiguity and demand of a project can
result in people resorting to reactive behavior. If
you haven't agreed upfront what of this behavior
is acceptable, clashes and conflict can arise."
—Karlijn Rademakers, Process Engineering
Department Manager Asia Pacific, China

The best time to agree on shared project values is before the
actual work on the project has started. Most projects start with a
project kick-off meeting, which offers a perfect setting for a workshop on shared values. You can be creative about how you want to
tackle the subject. You can use an assignment, exercise, or game to
work with the available group. Keep in mind the following targets
when getting creative:

- You need to understand what values the group finds
  important. Questions that may help you guide this process could be:

  ✓ What do we as a team stand for, in terms of values?

  ✓ What behavior should we practice?

  ✓ What behavior should not be tolerated?

- You need to reach agreement with the team on shared
  project values. Again, there is no magic number for
  the amount of project values you can agree upon. Just
  remember: less is more. Keep things simple, and make sure
  you yourself are also aligned with the values. You do not
  want to be the first one to not comply with them.

- Lastly, you need to find some way to physically agree upon the shared project values. It is not enough to just say you agree. You could have everyone sign a certain document, or maybe a project poster that you stick to the wall in a meeting room or office. Make a ritual out of it. This will help motivate everyone to stick to it.

Having agreed upon shared project values does not mean everyone will conform to them. During the entire lifespan of the project, it remains your responsibility to make sure that attitudes and behaviors stays aligned with the agreed-upon values. This is even more important when the pressure is on and tension rises. By making the shared project values a topic in periodic team meetings, or having a specific shared values meeting every now and then, you facilitate openness and accountability. You show that you remain committed to everyone walking the walk, instead of just talking the talk.

It might feel like a hassle on top of your already-busy meeting schedule. But keep in mind that most people want to work in a project environment where values are known, shared, and followed. They want to be in a setting where they feel trusted and can trust others, which will motivate them to go the extra mile. This will have a direct influence on the result of the project and your own performance, making the extra effort more than worth your while.

One of the project professionals I interviewed gave me the following example in relation to shared values differences:

"I was working on a project many years back, where there was a complete values misalignment with the lead engineer

from the customer team. This came to light when there where agreements made with him, mostly verbally, which he a few weeks later would categorically deny having ever happened. We spent time investigating if we could find some written support in emails or other documents to back up our stance, which we actually were able to do, but he still kept denying he had ever agreed to it.

We raised the concern of him not acting trustworthy, and a mediation was initiated. The collaboration went on after the mediation and did improve. However, the bad experience with him left a mark. People remained sensitive in communication and collaboration with him. The project was completed successfully, but it negatively affected the efficiency and effort it took to get there. After the project was finished, that particular lead engineer went into retirement."

The next element of this chapter involves understanding the impact of culture on behavior. In almost every chapter thus far, I have spoken about culture. Interpreting in communication is influenced by culture. How we perceive social interaction with others is influenced by culture. And values, too, are largely determined by it.

Culture

In Chapter 2, I defined culture as the perceived reality of an individual or group. This perceived reality consists of shared beliefs, values, and customs that the members of the cultural group use to interact with the world and with one another. We all are members of one or more cultural groups, whether by upbringing or by choice. Examples of cultural groups include societies, religions, generations, and social classes. We all develop our own individual cultural identity based on our membership in and the influences of cultural groups.

Cultural identity is designed within each person. As children, we get introduced to customs by interactions with our parents, our teachers, our friends, and others in the places we grow up. We learn how to act and react, what to see as good and bad, and what to perceive as normal and not normal. As we grow older, we get exposed to more and different sets of beliefs and customs, through which our cultural identity changes if we choose to embrace them.

Often, culture is believed to be defined by the foods, music, clothing, and social activities a group share. This is, however, a much too narrow interpretation. Culture is the combined thoughts, feelings, attitudes, beliefs, values, and behavior patterns shared among a group of people from diverse racial, ethnic, and social backgrounds.

Culture is dynamic, with people moving between cultures. A person might grow up in a poor, rural area and end up in adulthood in a more up-scale, urban life. Language might change from the area one grows up in to the language surrounding one later in life. Defined gender roles might shift if a person ends up in a more equal education or work setting than what they grew up in. These are only a few examples of the many culture shifts that could occur in a person's lifetime. Often, elements of the beliefs, values, and customs of one's childhood are retained and complemented with new elements from other cultures. Cultural identity development is an ongoing process of deliberate choices to adopt new elements of culture that were not part of our original upbringing.

We become most aware of the differences in culture during our interactions with others. We recognize during such interactions that we see, interpret, and evaluate things differently. What is considered appropriate behavior in one culture can be quite inappropriate in another. Often, we make assumptions of what is appropriate based on single cultural indicators, like race or ethnicity. In reality, a person's cultural identity is a complicated blend of all the cultural groups they belong to that have influenced their beliefs and behavior.

Much research has been done on what defines culture. According to Zion & Kozleski (2005), there are a number of basic elements present in our interactions, which result in patterns of behavior that are shared amongst cultural groups. Combine this with someone's personality or individual make-up, and the context of specific situations, and you get a better understanding of the beliefs, values, and norms of their everyday life. Some of these basic elements are the following:

- Language

I already emphasized the importance of taking away linguistic barriers in Chapter 2. It is important to understand that in different cultures, people use language differently, dependent on the people they are interacting with and the situations they are in. Think of formal versus informal language and the use of slang and dialect. Body language such as norms around hand gestures and eye contact differs between cultures as well. Where eye contact in European countries signifies interest and honesty, in Asian countries it can be perceived as an insult or attack on someone's authority. Have you ever noticed the many ways in which people use their hands when they talk? One of my colleagues from Latin America once mentioned that when he moved to the Netherlands, he was lost in terms of reading people's intentions. The Dutch do not use their hands as much as the

Latin Americans do, which led him to make the deliberate choice to develop and adapt his body-language skills.

- Attitude toward time

Being early, late, or on time has a very different meaning across various cultural groups. Some value living in the moment, while others structure their life through schedules and appointments. For some, being punctual is a sign of respect. In other cultures, setting a meeting time is just an approximate. Cultural groups do not necessarily equate to country borders. In the Netherlands, being punctual is a priority in the northern part of the country, while in the southern part, being fifteen minutes late for a meeting is quite okay. They even gave this a name, "het Brabants kwartiertje," which literally means "the Brabants fifteen minutes."

- Distance between individuals

The way people greet each other and the proximity in which they interact also differs between cultural groups. In some cultures, shaking hands is the norm, while in others, touching is a very personal act not to be shared among strangers. Norms can be governed by gender or relationship and might also apply to how close people stand when they interact. Invading someone's personal space is considered inappropriate in some cultures, while in others closeness between people is seen as a sign of connectivity and respect. This element can be very personal and not necessarily equal for all from the same cultural group. My partner, for instance, gets nervous when people enter his physical space, while I feel comfortable with a small physical distance.

- Gender roles

In most cultures, there is a difference in rules that govern the behavior of boys and girls. Many cultures believe that girls should be nice and quiet while boys should be assertive and loud. Other rules relate to expectations of future roles like marriage and having children or education for girls. I was taught at my Catholic primary school that the role of a girl is to have children. However, from an early age, I knew I did not desire to have children, which made me very conflicted in early adulthood. Have you ever considered what gender roles you were taught as a child? Have they changed during the course of your life?

- Taboos

There are many taboos in culture, and they differ between cultures. The Dutch find it inappropriate to walk into someone's office without knocking. In Germany, blowing your nose in public is a no-go. In Russia, it is a taboo to interact with someone while your hands are in your pockets. And in China, it is considered rude to not use both hands when exchanging business cards. It is key to know and understand the cultural taboos of the cultures you are interacting with.

- Grooming and presence

Consider your own response to meeting someone new who is dressed in a tailored suit and carefully styled hair. What assumptions do you make about this person? Clothing, grooming, dressing, and makeup styles vary based on culture. In some, it is appropriate to cover up flaws and accentuate positive features, while in others it could be considered bold and inappropriate.

- Autonomy

In some cultures, autonomy is a major influencer of personal motivation. In other cultures, the personal need for autonomy is subordinate to the needs of the collective. Individualistic cultures support individual gains and achievements, while collective cultures support the group—for instance, a family, religion, or nation. Have you ever noticed how people are introduced? Consider the following two examples to spot the difference:

- ✓ This is Rose. She has a degree in Law and currently works at Graham & Scott law firm.

- ✓ This is Peter. He is my neighbor Jake's son and went to law school with my niece Rose.

- Status of age

Some cultures are more hierarchical than others and show respect to older members of the group over younger members. Should children, for instance be "seen and not heard?" Should elders be addressed with "yes sir" or "yes ma'am?" Other cultures treat every member of the group with an equal amount of respect.

Other basic elements, according to Zion & Kozleski (2005), are familial roles, maturity levels, family ties, and education. All of them govern patterns of behavior that are shared among cultural groups and rooted in the beliefs, values, and norms of everyday life.

As a project manager, there is a strong probability your project will consist of people from a variety of cultural groups. We live in a world economy, which calls for international clients and suppliers. Easy migration of people leads to diversity in the workforce within countries and companies. In the role of project manager, it is therefore vital to understand the impact of cultural differences between people and learn how to appropriately deal with them.

One of the project professionals I interviewed gave me the following example in relation to cultural differences:

"I had the opportunity to go on an expat contract to Russia for two years. The program I was assigned to was run by a Russian program director and consisted of a number of smaller projects with designated project managers. I was one of them, working with a small team of natives and people of other nationalities to get things done. A cultural induction, which has become a standard in the years since, was not available then, so I kinda went in blank. Bad idea.

The first week working there, I was still busy introducing myself to the people on the site. During one of the days, I came into a big, open office space where a young lady was sitting at a desk. I went up to her to say hello and offered her a handshake. She reluctantly shook my hand before burying her face back into her work. I learned later on that this was an absolute no-go. A lady never touches the hand of a man in Russia. And it was in an open space, so everybody saw it as well. You can imagine how my reputation was already tainted by events the first week I was there.

Things only got worse after that. In the first meeting with the project director, I had a great idea for enhancing one of the strategies he suggested for my portion of the scope. As I was used to doing in my home culture, I suggested it to him in the meeting. This was not smart. He yelled at me in the meeting that I was just supposed to follow his lead and not interfere. It did not end there, as he ordered me into his office after the meeting, where the scolding continued.

Had I spent time on a culture induction before going to Russia, perhaps some of the cultural mishaps I ended up in would not have happened. It took me about six months to recover. Enlisting help from other expats helped me feel confident enough again in my own abilities to run the project."

There are several levels of understanding culture that reflect how we grow to perceive cultural differences.

- At the first level, people are aware of their way of doing things and see this way as the only way. They tend to ignore the impact of cultural differences. This level is called the parochial stage.

- At the second level, people are aware of other ways of doing things, but still see their way as the best. In this stage, differences are seen as problems to either ignore or reduce in significance. This level is called the ethnocentric stage.

- At the third level, people are aware of both their own way and the way of others. From both, they choose the best way appropriate for the situation they are in. At this stage, people are aware that cultural differences can lead to both problems and benefits. This level is called the synergetic stage.

— In the last and final stage, people create a culture of shared meaning, which meets the needs of the situation they are in. They embrace the differences between them and make new rules. This level is called the participatory third culture stage.

Successful cooperation is nearly impossible when people fear diversity. As a project manager it is therefore crucial for you to influence behavior in your project organization toward the synergetic or participatory stages. This influence starts with your own behavior and attitude toward differences. Then, you can start influencing the project team to also embrace diversity. Keep in mind the following when developing positive attitudes toward diversity:

▪ Identify feelings of diversity

It is important to facilitate and guide the exploration of feelings of diversity among the project team. Try to reveal the do's and dont's of the various cultures, so people can become aware and prepare for differences. You can find creative ways to facilitate a session as part of the project kick-off meeting and come back to it periodically in later project meetings.

▪ Refrain from judgement

Foster an environment in which people avoid judgement of one another over things they don't know anything about. Assumptions about a certain situation or certain behavior might be wrong; there is nothing wrong with accepting this. Set the example by articulating your own uncertainties, and come up with strategies on how to deal with them together.

▪ Embrace and celebrate diversity

Actively shape a project culture in which the ambiguity of the unknown is embraced instead of diminished. Show others the importance and beauty of diversity by setting the right example and rewarding appropriate behavior. During my time in Norway, I was given a peek into an initiative to celebrate diversity within an organization. This should help give you an idea of how to facilitate this:

Some years ago, I was working for a company in the Oil & Gas industry, managing the manufacturing of a specialized scope for a subsea oil field. The biggest chunk of the project had been procured from a company on the West coast of Norway. Due to a bad track record with this supplier, I was tasked with having regular onsite progress meetings with them. Each month, I would fly over for two days, during which I followed up on the progress of the scope.

During my two-day trips, lunch would be arranged by the supplier in the company canteen. This was usually a regular lunch with sandwiches, but I was lucky enough on a number of occasions to also be there the last Friday of the month, when it was culture day within the company. During these last Fridays of the month, the company would celebrate the variety of cultures of the employees working there.

The canteen would be decorated with customary decorations of the culture. The employee representing the culture would explain in front of the crowd more about where they came from and what the customs of their culture were. The company would provide a small budget for making traditional cultural food, which would be shared among the entire company for lunch. Participating in these Friday lunches, I had the privilege of eating kangaroo steak from Australia, and Borscht, which is a traditional beet soup from Russia. The ambience in the canteen was always positive and connected. It was a great way to take away the ambiguity of the unknown and celebrate diversity throughout the company. Can you come up with a way to celebrate diversity in your project organization as well? Try to be creative with it, and see what works.

At times, the influence of culture can be subtle; at others, its impact is unmistakable. Understanding the impact of culture on behavior within the project is vital to allow you to adequately deal with differences.

A project professional I interviewed shared with me the following exmaple in relation to cultural differences:

"I was working on a project with partners from Africa. We had regular video conferences and on-site meetings with them to talk about project progress. These meetings were attended by my counterparts as well as their senior management.

Reporting was put in a format in which it was almost impossible to raise concerns about challenges we faced. Raising them openly in a bigger forum with both my counterparts and their bosses attending would have immediately been seen as criticism causing me to lose reputation. The format made sure this would be avoided.

I didn't know this when I first started working on the project, though, and like in any other project, I raised my concerns at the meetings.

The reactions once I raised issues got really harsh. People were unwilling to cooperate, and the things I raised were immediately twisted into being my problem, not theirs. After a few meetings, I was told that concerns were being raised to the management at my company on how the meetings were going. After that, the entire project team got a sensitivity training, in which tools where introduced on how to communicate during these meetings. There was no quick and easy fix for the lack of issue-raising though.

In the end, I found a workaround, where I communicated directly and one-to-one with people instead of in a bigger forum. By raising things behind closed doors and in a personal manner, I could mitigate some of the risks to the project, but overall it turned out as a failure."

Another example from another professional:

"I was assigned as the account manager for a customer in Asia. Our company was running a multitude of projects with them, and they were very important to the company. I had been working in Asia for some time already and was introduced to the importance of maintaining a good relationship with them.

One of the first off-site meetings with them ended with a very exclusive dinner. I was the guest of honor and seated next to the owner of the company. It was difficult to talk much, as he spoke little English. We received a lot of very nice food, and during each course there was ample wine to go around. Every course and interaction with the owner started and ended with a toast, in which I felt obliged to drink my glass. After a while, I noticed that I was getting really drunk and wanted to stop drinking. I knew, however, it would be offensive to the owner to decline the drinks I was offered, so I kept on drinking.

The dinner ended late in the evening. I said my goodbyes before getting into a taxi with my colleague to go to the hotel. Only when I started moving did I notice how drunk I actually was. I remember reaching my hotel room and lying down. The next day, I woke up in the hospital. My colleague told me I had called him half an hour later to say something was wrong. He had found me unconscious in my hotel room and had called an ambulance. It turned out I had alcohol poisoning.

After this incident, I investigated how to deal with alcohol during business dinners. I was told it was not acceptable to decline a drink after having taken a couple of them already, that this was a loss of face. But declining drinks altogether with a good reasoning for it was okay. Saying upfront that, for instance, due to a medical issue I was not allowed to drink, would be a very legitimate reason to decline drinking without the host losing face. With this new strategy I have never been in trouble during business dinners again."

A final example:

"I had been assigned as an expat on a project in Aruba, which is part of the Dutch East Indies in the Caribbean. The scope consisted of consultancy work to upgrade the safety of a chemical plant. Together with the client, I made a list of short-, mid- and long-term improvements that should be done, and immediately steered work toward getting the short-term items done fast.

One of them was the construction of a small concrete wall to prevent spillage of chemicals in the event of an accident. I estimated the work to take four days, which took into consideration that perhaps things would be less efficient than I was used to. Just before I was to go on a three-week leave, the work on the wall had been subcontracted and was about to start. After three weeks, when I returned on site, the wall was still not completed. I wondered why and called the client in for a meeting to discuss. Apparently, one of the engineers designing the wall had fallen ill, and there had been no one available on the island to replace him. They managed to fly in someone from another location, but it took some time for this person to get up to speed. When the contractor finally received the drawings, it took a while to get the materials as well. I wasn't used to everything having to be transported by boat onto an island, like the concrete for instance. The example taught me to not assume I know how things work based on my experience. I work as much as I can with local people to get a good understanding of how things work before planning ahead."

"It is very important to accept everyone in the team as an individual person and not be biased against certain cultures. For this you need patience and tolerance."
—Philip Morgan, Project Buyer, Germany

Key takeaways

- Values are part of the deepest personal programming of humans and serve as general guidelines for behavior.

- Understanding your own values is key to living a full and authentic life.

- The bigger the overlap between individual and shared values, the better the performance.

- Every person has their own individual identity, which is largely influenced by the cultural groups they are part of throughout life.

- Shared patterns of behavior among culture groups consist of a number of basic elements: language, attitude toward time, distance between individuals, gender roles, taboos, grooming and presence, autonomy, status of age, and so on.

- Successful cooperation results from embracing diversity.

CHAPTER 6

MOTIVATE

lead
know
motivate
communicate
understand
socialize
adapt

After the industrial age, organizations tried to **motivate** their employees by focusing on managing productivity through set goals and an extrinsically driven reward system. This strategy resulted in a form of organized irresponsibility among employees. As a result, organizations introduced more and more goals and controls to try to ensure that employees did what was expected of them. Even today, organizations are introducing all sorts of effectiveness programs and new ways of working to increase responsible behavior. Unfortunately, those programs are often based on the implementation of logic and error-free execution.

"Motivation will almost always beat mere talent."
—Norman Augustine

The most complete view of humanity, however, shows people to be curious, vital and self-motivated. At their very best, they are inspired and thrive to learn. They extend themselves by mastering new skills, which they apply responsibly. Yet it is also clear that this spirit can be diminished or crushed, as observed in the millions of children and adults who stare blankly from the back of the classroom or wait lazily for the weekend as they go about their jobs. The proactive and positive tendencies of human nature are clearly not constant and can be motivated. Let us look at how.

Motivation is a variation of the word 'motive,' which in the The Collins English dictionary means "a source of energy for producing a motion," or simply put, doing something. Reasons in this case could be needs, desires, or wants. Science is not unified on what these needs, desires, and wants are. Some of the earliest motivation theories hold that human behavior, i.e. what people do, is based on satisfying a hierarchy of needs. Abraham Maslow for instance, in his book A Theory of Human Motivation (1943) explains that people are moved into action by unsatisfied needs, which are categorized in five hierarchical classes. People advance to the next level of needs only after the lower one is at least minimally satisfied. According to Maslow, the higher up the hierarchy a person progresses, the more individuality and psychological health this person will show.

Although Maslow's hierarchy of needs has become a very popular and often-cited theory of human motivation, it lacks scientific evidence. The few major studies that have been completed seem to support that there are only three levels of human needs. W. James (1892), for instance, concluded the levels are Material (physiological, safety), Social (belongingness, esteem) and Spiritual. Mathes (1981) proposed the three levels as Physiological, Belonging, and Self-Actualization. And Alderfer (1972) introduced Existence, Relatedness, and Growth in his ERG theory. Other theories express humans as being rational and guided by reason, or that motivation is a result of the participation in an action or activity as part of a cultural or social setting.

Science does seem to agree that the aspect of personality also plays a major role in the reasoning behind why people are motivated to do something. One of the most commonly used personality dimensions in motivation is that of introversion versus extroversion. Introversion means the motive for doing something comes from the

satisfaction of doing an activity itself, and is associated with self-motivation or intrinsic motivation. Some examples are achievement, recognition, responsibility, and advancement. Extroversion can be described as doing something for the reason of attaining a specific outcome, and is associated with extrinsic motivation. Some examples are pay, working conditions, physical surroundings, job security, and relations.

Motivation as a tool is highly valued in the modern world, as it has one major consequence: motivation produces. Motivated people are crucial to increasing productivity and quality within an organization. They bring about higher levels of output, allowing effective achievement of set goals. They positively influence the organization's culture, which in return leads to better retention, and so on. Motivation pays off.

The challenge many leaders and managers face is how to create the kind of motivation that produces. As a project manager, you know that within most projects you face the additional challenge of the often-lacking full-time involvement of team members. Matter experts work on different phases of the project and are often members of multiple project teams, with each project manager competing for their time and allegiance.

However, an ill-motivated project team has been known to entangle even the best project plan. As a project manager, you need to be able to utilize the initial excitement of starting a new project and use it throughout the project to drive performance. Although you can't control everyone's ambition, you can control the way you conduct your project and engage with everyone to generate more enthusiasm. It is up to you to find ways to motivate everyone to overcome obstacles and stay focused, especially in those times when things do not go as planned, which in projects is the norm rather than the exception.

At this point, there seems to be little agreement on the identification and ordering of human needs, desires, and personality when it comes to motivation. Although there is much work to be done, there are tools available that are commonly used in business today. They are based on the previously mentioned theories like Maslow's hierarchy of needs (1954) and Alderfer's ERG theory (1972). People also use the four-drive theory of human nature by Nohria, Lawrence and Wilson (2001), or the self-determination theory by Ryan & Deci (2000). Do some investigation and see what the differences are. Meanwhile, I will give you two suggestions on how to increase your ability to motivate your project team instantly.

The easiest and maybe smartest way to determine what motivates the people in your project team is to simply ask them. Rather than relying on tools based on unsupported theories, you go directly to the source of the individual needs, wants, and desires. You simply ask people why they get up and go to work in the morning. If you are up for it, have someone imagine what work would be like if time and money were not obstacles. What would they do now, in a week from now, or in six months, if they had all the money and time to do what really made them happy? With additional questions, you can identify what is required to get engaged and committed behavior towars the role and activities at hand.

> One of the project professionals I interviewed gave me the following example:
>
> *"I was working on a project where one of the team members came in one morning completely upset. I tried to ask what was going on, but he wouldn't say. I heard from others it had something to do with his private life, his relationship or such. During the next couple of days, the person came in, but didn't really get anything done. I did not know how to handle it, but at one point I decided to sit down and ask what he needed from me or the team to help him with what was going on. Based on his answer, I was able to make some small adjustments that resulted in the impact of his situation being minimal to the project. After a couple of weeks, he came into my office to thank me for the space and time he'd gotten to deal with things.*
>
> *Since that time, I do not take for granted the impact I can have on the satisfying of basic needs. I make a habit of checking if people are doing well by asking them and helping out if I can. Only then do I have the opportunity to influence their professional performance as well. Motivation-wise, this strategy has worked well for me."*

However, if you do like a framework to get you started, I'd like to introduce the model by Ryan and Deci (2000). According to their self-determination theory, there are three ingredients essential to enhancing motivation. Ryan and Deci argue, first, that events which promote feelings of competence during activities will enhance motivation. For example, positive performance feedback stimulates motivation, while demeaning evaluations diminish it. The feeling of competence alone will not enhance motivation unless it is accompanied by a sense of autonomy. Choice and opportunities for self-direction all enhance a sense of autonomy and influence motivation. Lastly, relatedness is an essential ingredient. Humans are evolutionarily wired to feel more comfortable as part of a group or community in which their needs and opinions are valued and protected. Relatedness does not seem to be a necessity for motivation to be present, but a secure relational base seems to be important for the expression of motivation.

When someone feels competent, they have a sense of being capable of tackling the task or challenge they encounter. This feeling of **competence** can be stimulated. Keep in mind the following strategies when stimulating competence in your team members:

- Don't do everything yourself. Take a step back every now and then, and provide challenges for team members to step up and out of their comfort zone. It promotes a sense of competence and usefulness among your team. As an example, one of the project professionals I interviewed introduced in his team the opportunity to present the status of the scope under their responsibility as part of the weekly project meeting. He did not force anyone to do so, but only provided the opportunity. While some were quick to take on the new challenge, a few others never stepped up to the plate. It allowed the project manager to quickly identify individual drivers among his team and influence them accordingly.

- Don't rush to the rescue, even if you think the strategy to solve the issue at hand could be more efficient or the predicted outcome could be better. If it does not cause exposure or significant risk to the project, let it go. This will promote resilience and problem-solving among your team.

- No one can get good at anything if they are not willing to experience some failure. Learning to tolerate mistakes by making them transparent is a good strategy to promote the willingness to develop among your team. As an example, some years ago I incorporated lessons learned as an agenda point in every weekly project meeting. I introduced a weekly roster in which team members were tasked with presenting a case in which they themselves made a mistake and explaining how they solved it. Although it caused some negativity and resistance at first, in the long run it fostered a culture of inclusiveness and learning among the team.

- Focus on effort as opposed to outcome. Putting too much focus on the perfect end result makes people less willing to try, make mistakes, practice, and struggle to get better. Acknowledge the time, effort, and attempts that were made to deal with the challenge instead of just focusing on how it turned out. This promotes will-ingness to put forth effort the next time.

Does the above resonate with you? Are you perhaps already using some of the above to motivate the team? If not, take small steps in implementing the above or other strategies to stimulate competence, and see how they work for you and the team.

The next ingredient to stimulate intrinsic motivation is **autonomy**. No one wants to be told what to do at every turn, and no one wants to feel like they are babysitting. That's where balanced autonomy comes into play. In a practical sense, autonomy is about self-determination. It is the ability to direct how you live your life based on your own personal beliefs and preferences. In a work setting, it does not mean doing whatever you like. If you are employed, your organization or manager defines the boundaries of your control and decision-making power, creating an environment in which you can choose how autonomous you wish to be. This is the same for the project manager and team. According to Ryan & Deci, the more autonomy you can provide to the team, the more intrinsically motivated they will be/get. Keep in mind the following when stimulating autonomy among your team:

- Create choice within boundaries. The freedom of choice is a key element in autonomy, but too much choice can be detrimental. Firm boundaries and a system to hold people accountable for results are essential for autonomy to thrive. Within clear boundaries, the team will feel empowered to determine how to accomplish the tasks and challenges at hand.

- Grant the team ownership. Ownership occurs when you allow someone else to feel like something is theirs, not by delegating a task. I know this can be a tough balance when in the end the responsibility of project success remains with you as the project manager. However, letting a team member feel like they have ownership over a certain topic or challenge will inevitably help them to stay motivate toward achieving the project goals.

- Provide tools to reach goals. Make sure your team has the tools and resources they need to reach your goals, and theirs. Training, technology, additional hands—whatever freedom you have within the project boundaries will help. It says you are willing to invest in your team and their ideas, because you believe they will make it worthwhile.

- Provide feedback directed at personal growth on approaches and solutions that are taken. Encouraging others to do the same creates an environment of continuous learning

One of the project professionals I interviewed gave me the following example when talking about motivating through competence and autonomy:

"Many years ago, I was working on a project which was sold on a very aggressive schedule at the time. We had our standard schedule—everything was planned around that, and we were late on everything. I had to find creative ways to meet the contractual date, and we did. The scope included a specialized product from a single source supplier, which had a very long lead time. It was very important to reduce any project work related to this scope, as it would immediately have a positive effect on the overall schedule. The Functional Design Specification (FDS) holding all requirements for a product usually takes months to get approved. Long review cycles and new comments usually make this a tedious process, which was something we could not accept for this project.

The FDS for the specialized product needed to be created within four days around Easter. The project engineer who was assigned to make the document was sick two out of the four days available, making it almost impossible to get the work done in time. We went for it anyway. We did a thorough kick-off, and I made sure he understood I was there to support him with anything he needed. I made myself available to check on him regularly. Two days later, the document had been produced. The content had been checked with the supplier, and the document had been approved by the client. I was able to send it out just before the Easter break started. It was a great win for the project and I made sure the engineer got the recognition he deserved for making it happen. Only later did it come to my attention that the engineer was generally considered to be extremely slow and that some of the other project managers did not want to work with him.

I work well with people who are considered difficult. I make a habit of asking and recognizing what drives them so I can tap into it. For me, it is also important to create, within the boundaries of my authority, an environment in which they work well instead of molding them to the environment we are in. If this means having someone come in late and work longer in the evening, or even having them work remotely for a while, that is fine with me. The commitment to the successful outcome of the project and delivery on their promises is more important to me than sticking to the standard."

The third ingredient in the theory by Ryan and Deci (2000) is **relatedness**. Although, according to the theory, relatedness is not a direct contributor to intrinsic motivation, it does provide a platform for sharing emotions. I am a strong believer that the expression of enthusiasm and commitment among a team fosters inclusiveness and camaraderie. Therefore, relatedness, as an element of intrinsic motivation, should get your attention as well. Keep in mind the following when stimulating relatedness:

- Gatherings of the project team help define team membership and reinforce a collective identity. This should start with the team kick-off at the beginning of the project. Try to do something together, even without an allocated budget for a team-building activity or dinner. It will significantly reinforce the sense of being a team working on something together.

- The kick-off meeting is also a great way of introducing the team to symbolic actions or rituals specific to the project. Again, this is a great contributor to a unique team culture.

- Ensure you set up regular team meetings that provide a platform for communication of project information. During these meetings, team members can see that they are not working alone, that they are part of a larger team, that their efforts are part of a bigger picture—achieving the project goals together.

- The success of your project is the total sum of the micro-successes during its timespan. Celebrating these micro-successes or milestones is key in maintaining a positive work environment among the team. Give gratitude for success often, and don't forget to get

personal. It will keep your team engaged and committed. As an example, since moving back to the Netherlands, I regularly take small cakes to work, made by my sister-in-law who is a pastry chef, to celebrate success. I incorporate the company logo or pictures of events or people I want to celebrate. It takes me perhaps an hour and a half to organize in my personal time, but it has proven to be a big influence in creating a positive team culture.

> "If someone said to me, 'I am going to raise your salary by a thousand euros a month,' I would say 'Thank you very much' but wouldn't necessarily be much more motivated by it. However, someone taking the time to say, 'Thank you for doing a good job,' saying they appreciate the extra mile, this is a great motivator."
> —Philip Morgan, Project Buyer, Germany

Can you come up with some examples of when you tried to positively influence engagement and commitment among your team? What were the results? Take small steps. A culture of commitment and engagement does not happen overnight.

One of the project professionals I interviewed shared the following example of a team kick-off with me:

"During my weekly department meeting, I got assigned to a new project as a controller. It was with a project manager I had not worked with before, and I was curious to get to know her. A few days later, I received an invitation to attend the project kick-off. To my surprise, the location was listed as a hotel in the middle of the city. I had to be there at ten in the morning that following Monday.

On arrival, I was informed where to put my coat and bag and got directed into the kitchen of the hotel. The project manager was there to welcome me. She handed me an apron, which had the project name and a small logo on it. She asked me to put it on, get myself a coffee, and wait for everyone to arrive.

When everyone was there, she took center stage to kick off the day and the project. She explained a bit about the scope of the project, the customer who hired us to complete the scope, and the grand end-goal she had in mind to achieve success with the project. One of the ways to achieve this was by becoming a strong team, which she wanted to kick off by us getting to know each other outside the office setting. She arranged for us to work together preparing our own lunch before later on going into the more formal part of the kick-off, discussing items like the schedule, budget, risks, and so on. The day turned out to be great fun.

*Over the following days, when I met some of my col-
leagues in the mornings, we had a quick chat first about
the cooking experience, but later about other things as
well. I noticed that it was very easy to work with all of
them from the get-go. We had quickly established a relationship in which it was easy to share concerns and ideas.
We worked together for almost a year on the project, and
in the end achieved the grand end-goal. Aside from my
positive feelings over achieving project success, I also had
a lot of fun working on this particular project."*

There are some common mistakes as well when trying to motivate. I
have listed a few of them below. Think about them when you explore
how to motivate the people involved in your project:

- "Whatever motivates me will also motivate others."

Don't get caught in the trap of perception that what drives you also
drives others. These drives might be similar, but usually this attitude results in disappointment, with people not reacting well to it.
Start with a more personalized approach—identify individual needs,
desires, and wants first.

- "I only work with professionals. They don't need
  motivating."

Not everyone is a self-starter or naturally driven to perform to the
best of their abilities. Most people, maybe yourself as well, work
better when motivated to reach a goal. Try to foster an environment
of motivation by using the tools or rewards available within your
authority and the limits of the project.

- "I'll motivate when there is an issue."

Waiting for a problem before stimulating motivation will most likely result in a request for behavioral change in times when pressure is already on. Not everyone will respond well to this, making the stimuli counterproductive to what you are trying to achieve. Throughout the project, maintain focus on the group as well as the individual needs, desires, and wants.

- "People love to receive public praise"

Although the phrase "praise in public, punish in private" is commonly used among managers, be mindful of letting it guide you. Not everyone likes the spotlight, not even for praise. Make sure upfront that the person deserving praise is okay with a public acceptance, or just take a safer approach by publicly rewarding the team effort instead.

These are only a few of the mistakes you can make when attempting to motivate your project team. Be conscious of what happens when you try a new approach. In the beginning, it will be trial and error. But as you get more experienced, you will see that you get better at it. Don't lose track of the endgame; an engaged and committed team will help you reach the project goal(s), which will reflect positively on not just the performance of the project organization, but also on your own performance as project manager.

"I am convinced you can motivate others. It's all about the story you tell, about being a storyteller. When you can reach them so they can see the sense of it, they can be motivated."
—Phillipe Morelle, Projects, Construction & HSE Manager, Belgium

Lastly, I want to share with you the work of Liz Wiseman, an American researcher and author. She conducted research into leadership, and states that there are two types of leaders: the multipliers and the diminishers. The first believe people are naturally smart and capable, that their role is to cultivate what is already there to create a multiplying effect within the individual and team. The latter, on the other hand, believe that true intellect is scarce, and that without their help, people will not accomplish what is needed.

Wizeman concludes that a surprisingly large number of diminishers are unaware of the effect they have on the people around them. They often climbed the corporate ladder based on their accomplishments and are praised for their intellect. Aside from the common mistakes, which I made you aware of on the previous pages, the work by Wizeman is a great enhancement to understanding any negative effect you might have on the motivation of the project team.

Key takeaways

- Individual motivation is a result of the satisfying of needs and personality.

- The easiest way to uncover individual drivers is by asking.

- It is useful to create a motivational framework that applies competence, autonomy and relatedness for motivation.

- It is as easy to enhance as to diminish motivation in others.

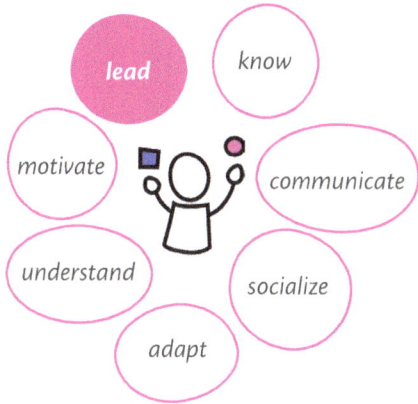

CHAPTER 7

LEAD

Each day, stories appear in the newspapers discussing instances of successful **leadership,** as well as significant failures. These stories usually concern national politicians or statesmen, chief executive officers of business and industry, or generals and admirals. But leadership is not just the responsibility of the people at the top. Leadership can occur at all levels and by any individual. This is the case with projects as well.

Although the title of project manager implies you should be more of a manager than a leader, the skills of the People Factor so far can all be attributed to leadership instead of management. As a leader, you need to know your own strengths and weaknesses, as well as those of others. You are in constant interactions in which you build relationships with the people around you to motivate them and gain support to reach the project goals. You make use of your understanding of differences in people and situations and adapt to whatever the project throws at you. You lead the project people, project process, and project content, to the desired target: the successful project outcome.

There are still some topics missing from the People Factor, though, topics that were uncovered through my research and the

subsequent interviews I conducted with practicing project professionals. In this final chapter, these topics will be reviewed.

Create a Vision

During a business trip in 2010, I was lucky
enough to be in the presence of the oldest
of the seven wonders of the ancient world,
located in the Valley of the Kings in Egypt. I marveled
at the great pyramid of Giza as I stood at the base of
its enormous structure. Research estimates it's almost
150-meter-high construction occurred somewhere around 2500 BC.
There is compelling evidence that the workforce consisted of thou-
sands of tradesmen and paid laborers instead of slaves. Over the
period of two decades, workers moved and erected an estimated 1.3
million stones to complete the structure that is still standing strong
today.

At the base of the pyramid, in the souring Egyptian sun, I could not help but wonder what had been needed to complete this marvel. Top-notch engineering for sure, but what about getting the people committed to its completion? There must have been construction accidents and diseases among the workforce. Still, the pyramids were completed at an astonishing speed. Scripture teaches us that people wanted to contribute to these great architectural wonders and saw their importance in national pride and religion. They committed to something greater than themselves, because they believed in the splendor it could become. They were compelled by its vision.

Going back to the beginning of the book, the engine of almost any organization in the world today runs on a combination of business as usual and projects. Projects are classified as being strategic, operational, or sales projects, and all of them contribute to the sustainability of an organization. If a decision is made to make budget and resources available to execute a project, it is because in one way or another, the outcome of the project is going to contribute to the overall business. Each project, therefore, has a business goal or goals.

Common business goals are revenue, cost, efficiency, and productivity. All of them are vital to the longevity of an organization but aren't very compelling to its people. It is therefore key to translate the business goals into a compelling vision, whether for the whole organization or a specific project. A project vision involves the less-tangible aspects of performance. It is, simply put, a picture the project team holds in common about what the project will look like when it is completed. This picture is compelling and shared, resonating in the minds and hearts of the people working to achieve it. It is the responsibility of you as the project manager to establish this picture.

While the vision is a grand, encompassing idea with emotional weight, a slogan or symbol is its simplified representation. Do you know which companies use on next page?

Just do it!	Because you're worth it	Life's Good

"It is a fine line between creating a target picture which is very specific versus leaving enough room for interpretation. You want to find that space where the target is clear enough so that people can relate to it, but it also gives them some freedom to connect to it based on their own experiences. That's when it's the most powerful!"

—Bengt-Olof-Klemp, Managing Director, Germany

All these companies have translated their business goals into something people can relate to. They have translated their vision into a tangible statement and created a slogan or symbol (or both) for people to believe in and commit to. The above companies and slogans perhaps sound a bit far-fetched for you as a project manager to relate to within your project environment. But don't forget, people want to be part of something that has meaning, no matter how small of a meaning this might be in the grand scheme of things. Just imagine what creating the right mindset and commitment will do for the likelihood of your project being a success, and what this success could mean for you.

If you believe in your project and are excited about it, it's just a matter of translating this excitement into a vision statement, a slogan, and a symbol. Alternately, just start with the vision statement if you feel more comfortable with that. Here are some things to keep in mind when doing creative work on making a vision statement:

- Align your vision with the business goals. For this to happen, you need to first make sure you know exactly what the business goals are. From some of the project professionals I interviewed, this remained an ongoing struggle, where senior management either was not clear about what the goals were or kept changing them over time. It is your responsibility to make sure you know what the goals are and link them to the project vision.

- The vision needs to be simple. If you're writing a statement, you run the risk of it not being clear by using a lot of text. Remember: the vision needs to be easy to focus on and memorable; otherwise, achieving it is a lost cause.

- Have a time horizon. Deciding on a fixed point in the future when you will have achieved or re-evaluated your vision helps make it more tangible. Remember as well that if your project takes a number of years, there is no law stating you cannot create separate statements or slogans for smaller portions of the overarching project. It is all about making it tangible and relatable in order to create meaning and gain commitment from the project team.

- Be ambitious. Your vision should not be too easy to achieve, nor to challenging that it will be missed completely.

To reinforce the importance of alignment on the target of a project, below is an example by one of the project professionals I interviewed.

"I was working in the events industry together with a managing director for a theater. He enlisted two teams to prepare and manage the program for the new theater year. One team was tasked with providing the content for the program. The team I managed was responsible for mar-keting & communications to reach the customers of the

"If the project manager doesn't have clearly in-front of them where to go, and isn't able to communicate it properly, it is chaos!'
—Eilif Eide, Subsea Engineer, Norway

theater. I kicked off the project with a briefing by the managing director to establish the objectives for the new theater year. I assumed the process would be approached in a similar manner by the content project manager. Later on, I sat down with my team to translate the objectives into a strategy, after which we started working on a plan and roll-out.

After a couple of weeks, conflicts started arising between the content team and my team. My team had difficulties getting information from the other team to determine which communication channels to use. Questions like, 'What is the idea behind the content?' 'What is the target group?' and 'What people do you want to reach?' were not being answered. I set up a meeting with the content project manager to see what could be done. It became apparent quickly that she was working with a completely different set of goals than we were. She had not been briefed by the managing director on the objectives for the program, and she did not reach out to him herself to understand them.

The first thing I did was plan a meeting with the managing director, myself, and the content project manager. We spent an afternoon talking about the main objective of the new year and brainstorming on smaller objectives that both content and marketing & communication could agree and commit to. After this, the cooperation between the teams improved, and we managed to create a great program, which created big audiences and great reviews."

Be Approachable

The next topic related to leading is being approach-able. A number of project professionals I interviewed described this skill as crucial in achieving the project goal. As a project manager, you want to ensure you are visible and approachable so that you hear about ideas, issues, problems, and circumstances that would perhaps otherwise never come to light. You do not want to end up in a position where you are the last person to be aware, or where you miss out on an opportunity to change course because people aren't shar-ing. The speed at which information reaches you is determined by your approachability.

> "Project manager that are approachable get involved!"
> —Phillip Morgan, Project Buyer, Germany

According to The Collins English dic-tionary, being approachable means "being friendly and easy to talk to," and "being able to be reached from a particular direction or by a particular means." Although it doesn't necessarily mean being liked or accepted, both do help. Typically, early on in relationships, people will assess if you are an ally and can be trusted. If they can't get confirmation of this easily, they will come to quick conclusions that will be difficult to overcome.

Being approachable is something that should come very natu-rally to us. Babies tend to elicit spontaneous smiles and waves from strangers who have no problem approaching them. Somewhere along the way, we lose this ability, perhaps through difficult experi-ences or modeling by others.

Being approachable implies the ability to accommodate, to make others feel comfortable talking to you. If someone wants to approach you for the first time, this can feel quite stressful for them.

How are you going to react? What will you say? Will the person be satisfied after talking to you? You can alleviate some of this discomfort by
being more attentive, interested, and inquiring. This does not require
a complete personality overhaul. Small changes to your behavior can
already go a long way, as described in the example below:

*"I was working in a small, family-run business tasked with
running small sales projects delivering components to
larger manufacturing companies. I was completing most of
my projects within budget, but kept running into delivery
issues. We worked with one key steel part supplier, and the
parts I needed kept moving down the priority list, much to
my frustration. Although I kept stressing the urgency and
importance of my parts to the procurement department,
my parts managed to always come last. During a dinner
with a colleague one weekend, I was told I was not very
liked by the procurement department and was not getting
informed on time of when the weekly priority list was being
updated. I never got the opportunity to stress my urgency
until after the list was already done and sent to the supplier.
With this disadvantage, I would never be able to deliver my
projects on time.*

*The next week, I decided to make some adjustments. I
set myself the goal to make a deliberate effort to change
my relationship with the procurement department starting that day. At first, it was quite uncomfortable. Now
that I was taking notice, it was pretty obvious that they
did not like me much. which made me downright uncomfortable. But I stuck to it. I smiled, made small talk at the
coffee machine, went to lunch with some of them, and
approached them in a more positive manner when I had a*

project matter to discuss. At the end of the second month, I was approached by one of the ladies asking me what steel parts I needed with the highest priority for the next week. 'Mission complete,' I thought. It felt great being able to create trust between myself and the department again by just making a genuine effort. After trust was established, it was super easy for me to approach them and vice versa."

With only a few behavior adjustments, the project manager in the above example was able to become more approachable. It is up to you to break down any barriers there might be and create an environment of trust and confidence in your project. Keep in mind the following when developing your approachability:

- Smile

Cuddy (2010) conducted a study on first impressions. Your facial expressions largely influence people's initial impression when considering if you can be trusted. Smile—it's that simple.

- Look available

It seems obvious, but looking available is one of the most effective strategies you can use to break down physical barriers between you and the team. Not much says "don't approach me" more than sitting behind closed doors or staying at your desk all day. Get up and walk around. Use the informal time at the coffee machine or in the hallway to have a chat with people. You'll be amazed by how quickly people will start sharing.

- Take interest in others

Make a genuine effort to talk to and understand the team members. Find out what they do, check if they have what they need, and take action where necessary to support where things seem to go wrong. Remember, though, autonomy is a direct driver of motivation, so don't overdo it. Don't run to the rescue and do everything yourself.

- Create pathways to you

It is one thing to say you are available, quite another to facilitate easy access to you. Tell everyone involved in the project how to contact you, and not just when there are problems. Be transparent about when you are in and out of meetings by sharing your calendar.

- Be visible

If you are never there, you also won't be approached. With the flexibility of work these days, you or the team might not be in one location all the time. Try to set up days or times when everyone is connected, whether physically or digitally. This will go a long way to the sharing of information.

- Create an atmosphere of sharing

An atmosphere of sharing starts with yourself. An unwillingness to share your own ideas and thoughts discourages willingness to share among others. Reserve time in meetings for sharing ideas, input, and thoughts. Encourage the team to share by sharing yourself. Don't forget to update them on project details as well. There is no such thing as oversharing in this case. Talk about progress and delays, risks and opportunities, successes and learnings, and the client.

I have an experience I would like to share with you from a manager of projects, whom I used to report to for some years:

"When I started working at the company, all the employees were located at a portacabin park on-site during the construction of a brand new office building. I was used to my manager's office being like any office I was familiar with: a big desk for him and two chairs in front of the desk for others to sit at. I am sure you have seen a gazillion offices like this as well, right?

After a year, it was time to move. The new building had a whole lot of excellent new features, and I loved it. I remember getting into my manager's office for the first time, however, and being less positively surprised. He had replaced his big desk with a tiny table in the corner of the room, which had his computer and chair. Then there was one big table with eight chairs around it, placed in the middle of the room as the centerpiece. My first meeting with him was strange, to say the least.

As time went by I never really thought much about the little desk in the corner of the office. But when I started investigating approachability as a skill, it came back to me again. I to-date still find it very innovative to put the conversation with others centerstage in your own office as opposed to having the most comfortable amount of space to sit and work at for yourself."

"You want people to not only limit themselves to the tasks at hand but to take co-ownership of the success of the entire project. For this, you need to be open to anything they want to share with you."
—Marlene van Benthum, Coordinator Soroptimist International LAB Development, The Netherlands

One of the project professionals I spoke with gave me the following example of the influence of approachability:

"I was working as an engineer on a project where the project manager was extremely busy. He was in the office one day a week, and when he was there, he would mostly sit in meetings or in his office with the door closed. He was physically less approachable, and his behavior did little to compensate either. If in the weekly meeting, someone raised concerns or brought up ideas, he would show no interest and make it clear to everyone that he had no time for anything else but getting the project completed quickly.

Although I don't recall myself having major issues because of this project manager, I don't really like working like this. It is demotivating to have the feeling of being on an island by yourself, with no one to go to for support. If a project manager is approachable and able to listen and support, I definitely feel more willing and obliged to go the extra mile!"

Key takeaways

■ A target picture that is compelling and shared resonates in the minds and hearts of the people.

■ Translate your belief and excitement into something others can commit to.

■ The sharing of ideas, issues, problems, and circumstances starts with your approachability.

■ An atmosphere of sharing starts with you sharing yourself.

AFTERWORD

Projects, in one form or another, have been around for as long as humans have been. They've existed as endeavors in many shapes and sizes, bringing together people and a vision to accomplish something unique.

Since the 1950s, the development of project management best practices has revolved around the rational and tangible parts of projects. Teams of professionals armed with a budget, schedule, scope breakdown, metrics dashboard, and so on are deployed with the responsibility to achieve project goals. Reality teaches us, however, that a staggering amount of projects in many industries fail to meet expectations.

Organizations worldwide keep expanding the use of projects as methods to increase stability and sustainability. Project professionals are hired on the basis of having received formal training in the rational and tangible "whats" and "hows." Or, they are being sent off to training to learn to use them. Even though research teaches us that the skills taught are not enough to make a project successful on their own.

I wrote this book to create awareness among both organizations and professionals that there is a way to significantly increase the low probability of project success. The seven skills I've introduced as the People Factor are all mission-critical project skills to possess. Each chapter acts as a guideline to help you develop the skill to know, communicate, socialize, control, adapt, understand, motivate, and lead.

Once you command the skills of the People Factor, together with the already available rational and logical "whats" and "hows," you have equipped yourself to get things done. And through this, you will not only accomplish the project goals, but also your own goals!

The seven skills of the People Factor are not an exhaustive list. Nor are the composition and details of each skill. This framework is based on five years of research, and it will be expanded upon as I keep investigating. I have remained vigilant in collecting insights and thoughts that have not made it into the book yet, but that need further investigating. Some of them are too important to not acknowledge before ending the book.

Firstly, according to some of the project professionals I interviewed, the requirement for the amount of traditional best practices and people skills differs per project. A natural categorization emerged from these conversations, dividing projects into three levels: easy, difficult, and complex.

Easy projects are characterized by a clearly specified scope, low budget, and short timeline. They are run by teams of only a few people, who make use of mostly traditional best practices to achieve project success.

Difficult projects are characterized by a significant scope and large budget, which is executed over a longer period of time. Teams consist of a large amount of people, both internal and external. For the execution of these projects, both traditional best practices and people skills are needed in order to achieve project success.

Lastly, complex projects have a specified target or outcome, but no defined scope. Complex projects work against a budget, but this is open for change over time. The end goal in time is not defined. Short-term milestones are used to track progress. Complex projects require an emphasis on people skills over traditional best practices.

Although I can agree to the categorization of projects into easy, difficult and complex, I tend to disagree with the perspective on required people skills. I believe whenever there are people, there is a need for people skills, even if there are only very few people. Even a project run by two needs a joint commitment to its outcome. And people want to work with others they can trust and have a connection with, even if it's just one or two others. My opinion on the matter does not suffice though—hence, the need for further investigation.

Secondly, I've spoken to many project professionals from technical industries, such as energy, engineering, construction, IT, and tech consultancy. All of these professionals recognize the lack of people focus in their industries and the need for development of people skills. I did not only speak to professionals from these technical industries, but also to, for instance, people in the healthcare sector. Project professionals from these sectors confirmed the importance of people skills, but also emphasized the development of traditional best practices in their field. I found this to be a very surprising find. As I mentioned in the introduction of the book, the demand for written-down project management methods stems from technical industries. Although this is where the very first best practices originated from, nowadays projects are used in many aspects of organizations and across many different industries. It seems, though, that the best practices founded and extensively used by technical industries have not systematically found their way into other industries yet. I find this very interesting and need to investigate this further as well.

Another insight I want to share with you is the chain of command within many large project organizations I've encountered. Within smaller companies, the project manager mostly has responsibility and authority over the people they work with within the project. They are able to hire and fire employees and are required to develop and review performance.

Within large project organizations, however, this is often not the case. The project manager in these organizations is responsible for the commitment of the people toward a successful project outcome, but has only minimal resources at their disposal when it comes to performance. Authority for hiring and firing, and responsibility for performance reviews, lie with the department manager or line manager. This puts the project manager in a very tough position, in which relationships with department or line managers become extremely important.

I have quite a few years of experience working in large project organizations in which I had no authority over the people in the project team. From this experience, I have formed the believe that utilization of people skills such as those featured in this book allows every project manager to achieve project success.

The last thought I want to leave you with is the significance of employment disruption due to the rapid advance of Artificial Intelligence. The field of computer science is devoted to creating machines capable of performing tasks that used to require human intelligence. Some say this could lead to mass job displacement; others believe it could liberate us from hideous jobs. Between the hype and the fear, however, is a reality that organizations and professionals need to adjust to, a reality that could require a completely different skillset.

Together with some of the project professionals I interviewed, I tried to imagine if and what effect the rapid advancement of Artificial Intelligence and roboticization could have on project jobs and their required skillset. I believe that projects will not be exempt from the rapid technological advancement, but that the complete replacement of project professionals by technology is not on the horizon either. Activities like the establishment of a schedule or budget, or the analyzing of risks, are much more easily replaced by Artificial Intelligence than the skills required to work together with people. The ability to enable someone to interact effectively with others, to build trust among people, and to form a genuine connection—these skills will only be in higher demand going forward. By reading this book and developing the skills in it, you have therefore not only set yourself up for project success, but also paved your pathway to a long and fruitful career!

After reading this book, if you would like to ask me a question or share your project experience, please register at www.members thepeoplefactor.nl. Please include the words "Talk to Sonja" in the registration form and proceed to send me a message. I commit to responding to you within 48 hours upon receipt. I look forward to talking to you!

To stay updated on the development of the People Factor and the People Factor Thinking, register for courses, or receive individual coaching, please visit my website: www.thepeoplefactor.nl.

Acknowledgements

Just as projects are joint efforts, so was the writing of this book. Everyone on this page has touched me or my project journey in a significant way, which I am ever grateful for.

Thank you to all the professionals I interviewed or had constructive conversations with during the course of the last five years:

Barbara Salopek, Annelies Meijers, Bengt-Olof Klemp, Tish Layton, Cynthia Soeters, Eilif Eide, Eunice Hammond-Mørklid, Henning Kohn, Jan Mollerup, Philip Morgan, Marlène van Benthum, Anastasios Kallias, Mirjam van der Plas, Niels Visser, Olivier Francescangeli, Pascal Stoer, Phillipe Morelle, Pierre Henquet, Ren Lin, Swetlana Thompson,

Yannick Avril, Sebastian Hennings, Marcin Wakuluk, Alek Cywinski, Sanne Smit, Arild Fotland, Henning Gresh, Antoine Adams, Seyyal van Schaijk, Edgar Wingo, Iris de Wilde, Sudhir Singh, Roel Scheepmakers, Ad Verschuren, Bas Cremers, Leen Streng, Wil Heijmans, Jolanda de Jonge, Taylor Drake, Marije Lafleur, Judith Oosterom, Mary Jane Roy, Irene de Kiewit, Daan van der Hoeven, Nettie Wester, Katherine Storoy, Nicoline Mulder, and Ellen Budde. If by accident I left you out of the above list, I sincerely apologize.

A thank you to *Maurits van Sambeek*, for keeping me on track during the entire writing process. It was a joy to meet up each week and laugh at your Southern jokes.

To *Judith Oosterom*, for not only sharing with me your project experiences, but also for providing me with the wonderful stick figures that grace the chapters of this book.

To *Jake Blok*, for that time at 'Oud London' when you told me to create, until look—there is a book! And for your trust.

To *Karlijn Rademakers*, for the fun and meaningful conversations we have wherever we go in the world. And for sharing the rollercoaster ride that was our first project together.

A special thanks to *Christo Nel* for your teachings, supervision, and guidance throughout all these years. I don't know if I would have gone on this journey without it. The grace with which you walk through life is an ever-present inspiration to dare.

And lastly, to my inner circle. My *parents* and *brother*, who have known me all my life and whom I call home. To my brother's little family and my baby niece, who is the apple to my eye. And finally to *Rob*, with whom I share my most inner thoughts and who never judges me.

Notes

Introduction

- Gillard, S., 'Soft Skills and Technical Expertise of Effective Project Managers' 2009.

- Gareis, R., & Heumann, M., 'Benchmarking the Project-oriented Society', 2015

- Larson E.W. and Gray C.F., 'Project Management, the managerial process', 2011.

- Seymour T. and Hussein S., 'The History of Project Management', International Journal of Management & Information Systems, 2014.

- Belzer K., 'Project Management: Still more art then science', 2001.

- Neuhauser C., 'Project managers leadership behaviors and frequency of use by female project managers', Project Management Journal, 2007 (page 21–31).

- Matthews D., 'Nasty 'surprises' cost reputations dear', raconteur. net, 2016.

- Mulder N., 'Value-based project management: an introduction', 2014.

- Mulcahy R., 'What makes a project manager successful?', 2002.

- Nel C., 'Leading transformation, the flying-wheel of sustainable change', 2018.

- Crowe A., '4 signs that you're a natural born project manager', 2014. Retrieved March 2019, from https://www.liquidplanner. com/blog/4-signs-that-youre-a-natural-born-project-manager/.

- Jewell B., 'Just how important are projects in today's organisations?', 2017. Retrieved April 2019,

from https://www.kent.edu/yourtrainingpartner/
just-how-important-are-projects-today's-organizations.

The People Factor – Chapter 1 – Know

- Collins J., 'Good to great', 2001.
- Lewis M., 'Self-knowledge and social development in early life', 1990.
- Turner, J. C., Hogg, M. A., Oakes, P. J., Reicher, S. D., & Wetherell, M. S., 'Rediscovering the social group: A self-categorisation theory', 1987.
- McAdams D.P., 'What do we know when we know a person?', Journal of Personality, 1995.
- McLeod S.A., 'Self concept' 2008. Retrieved March 2019, from https://www.simplypsychology.org/self-concept.html.
- The school of life, 'Know yourself', The book of life, Chapter 3. Retrieved March 2019, from https://www.theschooloflife.com/thebookoflife/know-yourself/.
- Ukleja M., '5 reflective questions to discover who you are and what you want', 2019. Retrieved March 2019, from https://www.success.com/5-reflective-questions-to-discover-who-you-are-and-what-you-want/.
- Kennedy T., "How self-reflection gives you a happier and more successful life, 2018. Retrieved March 2019, from https://www.lifehack.org/696285/how-self-reflection-gives-you-a-happier-and-more-successful-life.
- ACTPS Performance Framework, 'The art of feedback: giving, seeking and receiving feedback, 2013.
- McLeod S.A, 'Carl Rogers', 2014. Retrieved March 2019, from https://www.simplypsychology.org/carl-rogers.html.

- Halvorson H.G., 'No one understands you and what to do about it', 2015.
- Wiley, 'About everything DiSC: Theory and research. Retrieved April 2019, from https://www.everythingdisc.com/ EverythingDiSC/media/SiteFiles/Assets/History/Everything-DiSC-resources-aboutdisc.pdf.
- C. Nel, 'Five stages of group development', (2010). Unpublished paper.
- TMA method, TMA competency library. Retrieved April 2019, from http://www.competencylibrary.com.

The People Factor – Chapter 2 – Communicate

- Deep S.D., 'The communication experience in human relations', 1998.
- Oomkes F.R., 'Communicatieleer: een inleiding', 2013.
- Krauss R.M., ; 'The psychology of verbal communication', 2002.
- Sandoval V.A. & Adams S.H., 'Subtle skills for building rapport', FBI Law Enforcement Bulletin, 2011. Retrieved January 2019, from http://www.au.af.mil/au/awc/awcgate/fbi/nlp_interviewing.htm.
- skillsyouneed.com, 'Interpersonal skills'. Retrieved January 2019, from https://www.skillsyouneed.com/interpersonal-skills.html.
- Project Management Institute Inc, 'The high cost of low performance: the essential role of communications, 2013.
- Prossack A., 'These six communication styles should be in every leader's toolbox', 2018. Retrieved January 2019, from https://www.forbes.com/sites/ashiraprossack1/2018/07/31/these-6-communication-styles-should-be-in-every-leaders-toolbox/#442d7fd55fd7.

- Van Woerkum C.M.J., 'Sociologen over communicatie: Het begrip en verschijnsel communicatie in de sociologie', 1979.
- Centre for Mental Health in the workplace, 'Verbal vs. non-verbal communication', retrieved January 2019, from https://www.work-placestrategiesformentalhealth.com/mmhm/.
- Cuddy A., 'Your body language shapes who you are', 2012. Retrieved May 2019, from https://www.ted.com/talks/amy_cuddy_your_body_language_shapes_who_you_are?language=nl#t-287019
- TMA method, TMA competency library. Retrieved April 2019, from http://www.competencylibrary.com.
- Carney D., Cuddy, A.J.C., Yap A., 'Power posing: Brief nonverbal displays affect neuroendocrine levels and risk tolerance', 2010.

The People Factor – Chapter 3 – Socialize

- Snyder M. & Ickes W., 'Personality and social behavior', 1985.
- Kennedy-Moore E., "What are social skills? Helping children become comfortable and competent in social situations", 2011. Retrieved March 2019, from https://www.psychologytoday.com/us/blog/growing-friendships/201108/what-are-social-skills.
- Radke S., 'Acting social - neuroendocrine and clinical modulations of approach and decision behavior', 2014.
- Halvorson H.G., 'No one understands you and what to do about it', 2015.
- Granovetter M. 'Gettting a job: a study of contacts and careers', 1995.
- De Klerk S., 'The importance of networking as a management skill', 2009.

- TMA method, TMA competency library. Retrieved April 2019, from http://www.competencylibrary.com.

The People Factor – Chapter 4 – Adapt

- Gallo A., ' How to control your emotions during a difficult conversation', 2017.
- Wood H.L. & Ashton P., 'The factors of project complexity', 2015.
- San Cristóbal J.R., 'Complexity in project management', 2017.
- Dalcher, D, 'Adaptability in projects', 2013. Retrieved April 2019, from https://www.apm.org.uk/blog/adaptability-in-projects/ .
- TMA method, TMA competency library. Retrieved April 2019, from http://www.competencylibrary.com.

The People Factor – Chapter 5 – Understand

- Brown B., 'Dare to Lead: brave work, tough conversations, whole hearts' 2018.
- Gouceia V.V., Vione K.C., Milfont T.L. and Fisher R., 'Patterns of value change during the life span: Some evidence form a functional approach to value', 2015.
- Quappe S. & Cantatore G., 'What is cultural awareness, anyways? How do I build it?', 2005.
- Jeffrey S., '7 steps to discovering your personal core values'. Retrieved March 2019, from https://scottjeffrey.com/personal-core-values/.
- Blackman A., 'What are your personal values? How to define and live them', 2018. Retrieved March 2019, from https://business.tutsplus.com/tutorials/what-are-personal-values--cms-31561.
- McCombs School of Business, 'Values', 2019. Retrieved March 2019, from https://ethicsunwrapped.utexas.edu/glossary/values.

- Zion, S. & Kozleski E., 'Understanding culture', 2005.

The People Factor – Chapter 6 – Motivate

- Maslow A., 'A Theory of Human Motivation', Psychological review, 50, 370-396, 1943. Retrieved April 2019, from http://psychclassics.yorku.ca/Maslow/motivation.htm.

- James W.., 'Psychology: briefer course', 1892. Retrieved April 2019, from https://archive.org/details/psychologybriefe00willuoft/page/n5.

- Huitt W., 'Maslow's hierarchy of needs', Educational Psychology Interactive, 2007. Retrieved April 2019, from http://www.edpsycinteractive.org/topics/conation/maslow.html.

- Ryan R.M. and Deci E.L., 'Self-determination theory and the facilitation of intrinsic motivation, social development, and well-being', American Psychologist, 2000 (page 68 - 78);

- Beurkens N., 'Competence: The Key to Improving Self-Esteem, Reducing Resistance, Instilling Responsibility, and Promoting a Positive Mood in Children' 2016. Retrieved March 2019, from https://www.drbeurkens.com/competence-key-improving-self-esteem-reducing-resistance-instilling-responsibility-promoting-positive-mood-children/.

- Maylett T., '6 Ways to Encourage Autonomy With Your Employees', 2016. Retrieved March 2019, from https://www.entrepreneur.com/article/254030.

- Larson E.W. and Gray C.F., 'Project Management, the Managerial Process', 2011.

- Peterson T.M., 'Motivation: how to increase project team performance', Project management journal, Vol. 38, No. 4, pages 60-69, 2007.

- Young M.L., 'The importance of motivation in project management', 2011. Retrieved April 2019, from https://pmhut.com/the-importance-of-motivation-in-project-management.
- Wizeman L., 'Multipliers: Hoe de beste managers 2x meer uit hun teams halen', 2015.

The People Factor – Chapter 7 – Lead

- Lewis, J.P., 'Working together: 12 principles for achieving excellence in managing projects, teams and organisations', 2002.
- Hollands-Steck L., Kaufman K., Hollands J., & Steck L., 'The approachability factor: influencing relationships and getting results', 2015.

Afterword

- Russel R., 'Why soft skills are crucial in the age of AI', 2018.

www.ingramcontent.com/pod-product-compliance
Lightning Source LLC
Chambersburg PA
CBHW042314210326
41599CB00038B/7129